WOMEN OF FAITH™
STUDY GUIDE SERIES

ENCOURAGING ONE ANOTHER

FOREWORD BY

NICOLE JOHNSON

THOMAS NELSON PUBLISHERS
Nashville

Published by Thomas Nelson, Inc., P.O. Box 141000, Nashville, Tennessee, 37214.

Library of Congress Cataloging–in–Publication data is available.

ISBN 0–7852–5153–7

04 05 06 07 08–12 11 10 9 8 7

✦ CONTENTS ✦

✦ FOREWORD ✦

Who doesn't love throwing confetti up in the air? At weddings, or parties or on New Year's Eve, everyone wants something in their hands to throw. It's a way of lavishing our love on people. Whether it's paper, rice, or birdseed, it's a way of cheering others on. Confetti is a tangible expression of our intangible emotions. Like happiness you can see and throw someone's way.

Encouragement is to a relationship what confetti is to a party. It's light, refreshing, and fun. It's cheer you can throw someone's way. But even deeper, it is the assurance you are there, that you are standing behind them and supporting them. The time it takes to gather little pieces of love, grace, strength, and hope is well worth it when you see what happens as you shower those gifts on someone else. It's like spiritual confetti, and it's the ultimate encouragement.

But how can we encourage someone else when we feel so discouraged? Our temptation is to stand in the corner of the encouragement party. Just hang around the edges and observe everyone else having a good time. But that never works. It's not until we start throwing the confetti on others that we realize how much is landing on us!

As we encourage each other, the Father encourages us. The two are interwoven. As we release the confetti on returned prodigals, we weep as we remember the confetti He threw when we came home. When we help a friend carry her broken heart, our own heart feels a lot lighter. We can encourage others from the overflow of God's encouragement to us.

So what are you waiting for? Grab a handful of confetti and jump in! But be careful, you're liable to find little pieces of it stuck on your clothes for weeks!

—*Nicole Johnson*

✦ INTRODUCTION ✦

"I believe it's a mission that God himself has put in all of us. As believers, we do not live on an island. We are part of a great universe of people who are loved by God, and his desire is that, as his children, we care about others."

—Luci Swindoll

Sometimes we plod through life with our head down and our back bent under the weight of our load. We feel unimpressive, unkempt, unappreciated, and unneeded. We've put our hand to the plow, but the theme song that runs through our minds is, "The old gray mare, she ain't what she used to be." Day in and day out, we push along, struggling to put our shoulders into it, give it a little elbow grease, and keep a stiff upper lip. Joyless existence. Who wants to live that way—without some reassurance to lift our hearts and steady our hand?

God doesn't want to leave us staggering under such weight of discouragement. It's quite the opposite, really. Our Heavenly Father loves us so much He does His best to cheer us up and cheer us on. Did you know God planned ahead for all of your gloomy days? He knows just when you'll need a little lift, and has arranged for encouragement to be right there, waiting for you to discover it! You only need to know where to look. Encouragement comes from personal, little miracles—spirit–lifting blessings from His own hand. Encouragement comes from knowing His promises, and the faith that flourishes from believing them. Encouragement comes from fellow believers, as you reach out and touch one another's lives. God did not leave us to face life alone. He is with us always, and we are all in this thing together. So let's encourage each other along the way.

*"Think of ways to encourage
one another to outbursts
of love and good deeds."*

Hebrews 10:24 NLT

CHAPTER 1

GOD ENCOURAGES ME!

"BE ENCOURAGED, YOU WHO WORSHIP GOD."

Psalm 69:32 NCV

For our anniversary one year, my husband purchased tickets to a Broadway play at the downtown performing arts center. I had weeks to enjoy the anticipation of an evening out, and make sure every detail was taken care of. Grandma was enlisted to care for the children. We planned where to have dinner beforehand, and where to get dessert afterward. I bought a pair of strappy, black shoes and some sparkling new earrings to lend some zip to the "little black dress" hanging in the corner of my closet. When the big night came, I withdrew to my chambers to prepare for an evening at "the theater" (that simply *must* be said with a certain pinched, aristocratic accent). Though I prefer to primp and preen in private, my sleepy two–year–old son accompanied me

CLEARING ✦ THE ✦ COBWEBS

When would you say you need encouragement the most?

throughout my preparations. He oversaw my efforts solemnly, leaning back against the pillows on my bed with one finger in his mouth. I powdered, polished, perfumed, and pinned up, and when I was done, he popped his finger out of his mouth just long enough to say, "You're beautiful, Mama." Then back in went the finger.

I was thrilled by his sweet compliment. I hadn't really *needed* that encouragement. After all, I felt beautiful, and I was having a really good day already. But we don't need to be having a bad day to delight in a little bit of encouragement. Encouragement is always welcome, even on those days when we're in an upbeat frame of mind.

1. Who *doesn't* thrive on encouragement? Where does our encouragement come from, according to Romans 15:5?

How do we find God? Sometimes we search Him out, and sometimes He "finds" us. Every time we think of God it is because He first had us on His mind. So know that once you have invited Him to enter your life, you are on His mind and He is in your heart.

Patsy Clairmont

2. One of the greatest sources of encouragement in our lives comes from the fact that God is always with us. We are His children, and His Spirit touches our very soul. In Philippians 2:1, Paul asks a series of rhetorical questions that bring up some very good reasons for us to be encouraged. What are they?

3. God encourages us in more direct ways. What encouragement does David thank God for in Psalm 138:3?

4. What is another great source of encouragement in our lives, according to Hebrews 6:18?

5. What else can we take unexpected encouragement from, according to Hebrews 12:5?

> *I determined to do whatever it took to keep my spirits up. I took God at His word—that He would be with me and take care of me; that He'd go before me and straighten out the crooked places; that He'd be my comforter, friend, and great physician. Something about that choice had a rush in it for me. And edge. And excitement. Each day I couldn't wait to see what would happen.*
>
> Luci Swindoll

*H*ave you ever been to a little league baseball game? Kids with grass–stained knees, dusty bottoms, and batting helmets which continuously slip over their eyes, go through the motions of America's national pastime. Some of these kiddos are real go–getters, but others pick dandelions in left field and daydream at shortstop. We can't help but smile when watching them. It's almost as much fun to watch the parents in the stands, as it is to watch those kids out on the field. They're cheering on their little slugger for all they're worth.

"Atta boy!"

"You can do it!"

"Take your time!"

"Watch for your pitch!"

"Run! Run! Run!"

Can't you just imagine God upon His throne and Jesus seated at His right hand—even the angels are lined up, peering into the matters of mankind—and they're all cheering *us* on! Whether we're giving it our all, or daydreaming somewhere out in left field, they shower us with encouragement.

"Steady now!"

"You can do it!"

"Hang in there."

"That's my girl!"

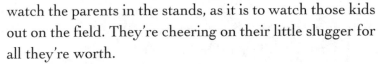

God is the all–knowing One who sees our scars, our secrets, and our strength. Our wounds and shame are His affair, and He knows just how much trouble we can stand. Somehow the fact that He knows us so well makes a difference. We understand there is a direction and we are part of a bigger picture. From the wilderness in our lives, the fact that He sees gives us a reason to carry on.

Barbara Johnson

6. Because our LORD encourages us, we are better able to give encouragement to those around us. When the well of our heart is dry, we have nothing to give, but God is able to fill our reservoirs to overflowing. What does Paul say in 2 Corinthians 1:6 about this?

7. What are we to do with all of this encouragement from God, according to Romans 15:5?

8. What is this "attitude of Christ Jesus"? Philippians 2:3–5 gives us a wonderful picture.

9. Our very lives depend upon the strength and encouragement God provides. How does Paul describe the bounty of blessings and encouragements we have been given in his benediction in 2 Thessalonians 2:17?

✦ DIGGING DEEPER ✦

In the New Testament, Jesus reached out and changed the lives of many people. He brought new strength and healing to those who were suffering, and He did it with just a touch and a kind word. Take a look at these two verses in Matthew, as they are translated in the *New Century Version*:

Some people brought to Jesus a man who was paralyzed and lying on a mat. When Jesus saw the faith of these people, he said to the paralyzed man, "Be encouraged, young man. Your sins are forgiven." —Matthew 9:2

Jesus turned and saw the woman and said, "Be encouraged, dear woman. You are made well because you believed." And the woman was healed from that moment on. —Matthew 9:22

Why do you suppose Jesus' first words to these two people were "Be encouraged"? What did they have to be encouraged about?

✦ PONDER & PRAY ✦

Many of the encouragements we need are already ours because they come from God's own hand. Pray this week for the eyes to see what has already been given. Even if there is no one else to come alongside you and encourage you during a difficult day, the God you serve will provide for your every need—even the need for encouragement.

✦ TRINKETS TO TREASURE ✦

At the close of every Women of Faith conference, women are asked to play a little game of pretend. Each conference guest is asked to imagine that a gift has been placed in her hands—one from each of the speakers—to serve as reminders of the different lessons shared. This study guide will carry on this tradition! At the close of each lesson, you will be presented with a small gift. Though imaginary, it will serve to remind you of the things you have learned. Think of it as a souvenir. Souvenirs are little trinkets we pick up on our journeys to remind us of where we have been. They keep us from forgetting the path we have traveled. Hide these little treasures in your heart, for as you ponder them, they will draw you closer to God.

✦ TRINKETS TO TREASURE ✦

Your first trinket of the study will be a reminder that God is always there, cheering you on. A baseball—just like the kind little leaguers would enjoy—can bring to mind the Host of Heaven, whose eyes are fixed on you. Can't you hear your Savior call, "Atta girl! You can do it!"

✦ NOTES & PRAYER REQUESTS ✦

CHAPTER 2

THE WORD ENCOURAGES

"I WILL THANK YOU FOR YOUR LOVE AND LOYALTY.
YOU HAVE MADE YOUR NAME AND YOUR WORD
GREATER THAN ANYTHING."

Psalm 138:2 NCV

Wouldn't you love to be a rustic, back to nature, hit the trails, rough–it kind of gal? I admire people who do just that: campers, hikers, naturalists, and survivalists. They are the kinds of people who can lose themselves in the woods for days at a time without worrying about food and shelter. They know how to pitch their tent and bank their fire. They know where the berries grow and which mushrooms are safe. They can tell a weed from a welcome addition to the soup pot. I admire them because I could walk along the very same trails, pass the very same plants and shrubs, and starve to death. I'd completely miss the plenty that nature provides, because I

CLEARING
+ THE +
COBWEBS

What ingredients would you put together to create the *perfect* trail mix?

wouldn't recognize it if it bit me! Once my trail mix ran out, I would not be a happy camper.

God has surrounded us with the means to be encouraged—little things throughout our day to lift our hearts. These are welcome tidbits, but unless we are tapping into God's Word on a daily basis, we are starving ourselves unnecessarily. The encouragement we receive from the Bible is real stick–to–your ribs stuff. It will stay with you, no matter how steep the trail in front of you gets.

1. Psalm 119 is an amazing chapter in the Bible. Nearly every verse sings the praises of God's Word. What does Psalm 119:28 say God's Word is able to accomplish?

God's Word will stand forever. It is more than an Old and New Testament compiled into sixty–six books that constitute a divine library. It is a source of guidance, strength, encouragement, and comfort, available every day of our lives.

Luci Swindoll

2. Encouragement is there for us, so long as we know how to find it. All it takes is our commitment to exploring God's Word. What does John say about the Bibles we hold in our hands in both John 20:31 and in 1 John 5:13?

3. Paul echoes John's words in Romans 15:4. What does he say the Scriptures were written for?

4. Paul understood the value of the Scriptures. What advice did he give to the young pastor Timothy in order to encourage his congregation in 1 Timothy 4:13?

5. What did Paul and Barnabas do to encourage the people in Acts 13:15?

When I was little, I hated most vegetables. I could tolerate sweet corn and the occasional green bean — carrot sticks and celery, if there was dip — but that's all. Still, my parents served up a plethora of good–for–me foods — asparagus, beets, peas, kohlrabi, broccoli, cauliflower, butternut squash, tomatoes, and zucchini. It was all I could do to choke some of it down. My Dad would always say, "We'll know you're grown up once you've learned to like them." I always thought that was a strange thing to say.

As a child, I thought sermons were dull. They were almost as bad as trying to eat my vegetables—just one more thing that's supposed to be good for me. Even if I *tried* to pay attention to the words of the pastor, I just couldn't see any point in the long, carefully outlined messages. Now my whole perspective has changed. My dad was right. I've learned to like them. Sunday morning sermons, Wednesday night Bible studies, Sunday school lessons, and daily reading—I can't get enough. Learning to love the Word came once I had grown up a bit. Though I still don't like squash.

6. Whether we are reading it for ourselves or sitting under good, solid preaching, God's Word can teach us "all things that pertain to life and godliness" (2 Pet. 1:3). All we need is a teachable heart. How does Job describe his willingness to be taught in Job 6:24?

> *Take a few minutes today to spend with Yahweh. Find the comfort and guidance you need from God's words of direction for that disturbing circumstance in your life. His words are there, and they're written just for you.*
>
> Luci Swindoll

7. God's Word encourages us to live in ways that would please God. What does David pray in Psalm 119:37?

8. What did Paul preach in Acts 14:15?

9. When we are teachable and willing to learn, God's Word is an effective tool for changing our lives, encouraging obedience and growth, and giving lasting joy and peace. *The Message* translates 2 Timothy 4:2, "so proclaim the Message with intensity; keep on your watch. Challenge, warn, and urge your people. Don't ever quit. Just keep it simple." How does your choice of Bible translation describe the working of the spoken Word?

✦ DIGGING DEEPER ✦

Let's take the time to seek out a few more verses empha-
sizing the importance of God's Word in our lives — and the
teachable attitude that must characterize our hearts. How
do these verses communicate this willingness to be
taught?

- Job 34:32
- Psalm 86:11
- Luke 11:1
- Psalm 25:4, 5
- Psalm 143:10

✦ PONDER & PRAY ✦

This week as you mull through the lesson, ask God to
show you just how much your life in God depends upon
His Word. As you deepen your appreciation for the
Scriptures, spend more and more time in its pages — even
if it means setting aside other tasks. In this way, you will
discover a vast store of encouragement.

✦ TRINKETS TO TREASURE ✦

Your trinket this week is trail mix. When you hit the trails
of life, you must be prepared. Knowing where to turn for
nourishment and shelter is vital. Make sure you remain a
happy camper in your day–to–day life by taking hold of
the encouragement found only in your Bible.

✦ NOTES & PRAYER REQUESTS ✦

✦ NOTES & PRAYER REQUESTS ✦

CHAPTER 3

ENCOURAGE MY FAITH

"I'M EAGER TO ENCOURAGE YOU IN YOUR FAITH, BUT I
ALSO WANT TO BE ENCOURAGED BY YOURS. IN THIS WAY,
EACH OF US WILL BE A BLESSING TO THE OTHER."

Romans 1:12 NLT

What kinds of things make you feel happy? Advertisers know! Why else would television commercials be filled with beautiful landscapes, spring flowers, clean sheets, cuddly puppies, close–knit families, colorful balloons, best friends, homecomings, contagious laughter, and silly antics? These images can really tug at your heartstrings. Admit it—you've actually cried over some of those old Hallmark commercials! We are easily influenced and even manipulated by our emotions.

We mostly think of encouragement as being a mood–lifter. It's that little compliment, a bouquet of flowers, an unexpected present, or a warm hug. But the encouragement God provides touches us more

CLEARING
✦ THE ✦
COBWEBS

I can remember the
Tootsie Roll® song,
the Oreo® song,
and the Big
Mac® song—
how about you?
Do you remember a
commercial jingle from
your childhood you
can still sing?

deeply than that. He doesn't offer a quick fix when our feelings get frazzled. What He's offering us is encouragement for our faith. If we are strong in the faith department, we are less likely to let our emotions drag us down.

1. Who are the people in your life who come immediately to mind when we talk about encouraging our faith?

> *Sometimes we need to be reminded of the great potential we possess. We need someone to point out our likeness to the One who created us, to see God's image in us. Just one little word of encouragement can make all the difference.*
>
> Barbara Johnson

2. We establish the faith of others when we affirm God's effectiveness working in our own life, and the lives of those around us. How does Paul describe this ministry in 1 Thessalonians 3:2?

3. Some people make it a full–time job to encourage the faith of other believers. We call those people who are in the ministry "full–time Christian workers." How are the ministries of two such men described in Acts 15:32?

4. Our pastors have a responsibility to encourage us in the faith. It is our responsibility to submit to their leadership—listening to them and heeding their words. How does Paul describe their work in Titus 2:15?

5. Those called to lead in the church must meet certain criteria—in this way, they are able to lead by example. But that doesn't let the rest of us off the hook—we should all aspire to lead such God–pleasing lives. How does Paul describe the ministry of encouragement a believer should have, according to Titus 1:9?

6. What is the greatest obstacle to encouraging one another's spiritual growth? Check in Hebrews 10:25.

> *That's the way of life, isn't it? We need each other. Scripture says two are better than one. We're instructed to love, pray for, care about, accept, forgive, serve, encourage, and build up one another.*
>
> Luci Swindoll

When you get together with your closest friends, what do you usually talk about? Do you talk about the weather, work, family, and the sales running right now at Wal–Mart®? We talk about shades of nail polish, next summer's vacation plans, new–fangled diets, spring wardrobes, fall fashions, and the price of a pound of hamburger. We talk about health problems, stress, in–law strains, disgruntled teenagers, and the newest grand-baby—we can hash them over for hours on end. We laugh over the old stories we share while catching up on old times. We swap recipes, recommend hairdressers, compare symptoms, and just generally have a good visit. And none of this is bad, in and of itself. But how can you encourage the faith of your sister in Christ if you never talk about the faith you share?

> I need to be drawn out of my own little world, and so do you. I see women all the time who seem joyless and lonely—I can see it in their expressionless eyes.
>
> Nicole Johnson

7. In a way, each and every believer has been called to preach the gospel. It was a part of the Great Commission. With this in mind, what does 1 Corinthians 9:14 tell us to do?

8. When Paul arrived in a church during his travels, he didn't waste any time encouraging the faith of those around him. How does he describe his efforts in Acts 20:20?

9. Encouragement goes both ways. You can encourage me, and I can encourage you. How does Paul put it in Romans 1:12?

> *I pray that what I learn from the lives of others will be used by God to make me a more compassionate woman, more willing to serve, more grateful to God and of more use to others.*
>
> Sheila Walsh

✦ DIGGING DEEPER ✦

This week we have focused on the encouragement of our faith. Did you know the Bible also urges believers to fight hard to protect their faith? Take a look at the little epistle of Jude. What do verses 3 and 4 encourage believers to do, and why? How is this applicable for us today?

✦ PONDER & PRAY ✦

This week, consider how much your faith has become a part of your life. Is it a nice tidy little bundle you manage to tuck into your Sundays and Wednesdays? Or does your faith touch every minute of your day? God wants to encourage you this week. Let Him lift your heart, but ask Him to strengthen your faith as well.

✦ TRINKETS TO TREASURE ✦

Your little treasure to take away this week is a gardener's trowel. It's to remind you to make the effort to dig a little deeper, and get past the surface chatter of our relationships. Consider your words carefully in the weeks ahead, and ask the LORD to help you bring conversations around to spiritual things. It may take a little effort to begin talking about your faith with those closest to you, but it will encourage their faith—and yours as well.

✦ Notes & Prayer Requests ✦

✦ NOTES & PRAYER REQUESTS ✦

CHAPTER 4

ENCOURAGING GROWTH

"AFTER SPENDING SOME TIME IN ANTIOCH, PAUL WENT BACK TO GALATIA AND PHRYGIA, VISITING ALL THE BELIEVERS, ENCOURAGING THEM AND HELPING THEM TO GROW IN THE LORD."

Acts 18:23 NLT

I t's pretty difficult to get your average chicken to follow you around. You can't exactly put them on a leash. Hens are easily distracted, stopping at frequent intervals to scratch and peck. Even if you get a few of them heading in the right direction, just one stepping off the path can turn the rest to wandering away again. Every grasshopper or butterfly that crosses the path incites a kind of chicken stampede. Hens really prefer to be free–range birds. If you try to catch them, they panic and run, clucking frantically. In fact, the only way to coax a hen to follow along steadily after you is to drop

CLEARING
✦ THE ✦
COBWEBS

Do you like to play "Follow the Leader" or "Simon Says"? Or would you rather do your own thing?

food for them in the path as you lead them along. A steady trail of breadcrumbs or corn kernels does the trick every time.

I realize the Bible says we are like sheep, but I'm kind of a chicken fan myself. God leads us along, even though we act like chickens. It doesn't take much to turn our heads or send us flapping in circles. So our Heavenly Father finds ways to coax us onto the path He wants for us to follow. As we walk in His ways, we discover kernels of encouragement He's scattered before us. Are these encouraging moments simply for our pleasure? No, they serve a purpose as well. They keep us headed in the right direction, and encourage us to grow in the directions He has planned.

1. We may not be quite as giddy as hens, but we need to know what we are chasing after and where our path will lead us. Take a look at the following verses:

- What does Paul tell us to pursue in Romans 14:19?

- What should we pursue, according to 1 Corinthians 14:1?

- What does 1 Thessalonians 5:15 say we should always pursue?

- What should the man of God pursue, according to Paul in 1 Timothy 6:11?

• According to Hebrews 12:14, what should we be pursuing and why?

2. Even if there is no other resource available to us, where can we find the encouragement to continue growing in the LORD? It's mentioned in Acts 9:31.

> *I thank God, and I thank that handful of loving folks who know what to say to me and how and when to say it, and for the fact that they do it kindly and in the spirit of grace. If you've got friends like that, praise God for them every day of your life. You are rich.*
>
> Luci Swindoll

3. How does Paul describe the efforts of his ministry team to ensure the growth of God's people in 1 Thessalonians 2:12?

4. What do we need in order to grow, according to 1 Peter 2:2?

5. Growing up in the LORD means what, according to 2 Peter 3:18?

> *What wonders a bit of encouragement can do! It's one of the most awesome treasures God has given us—the ability to inspire, motivate, and reassure others.*
>
> Barbara Johnson

6. How does this "growing up" appear in our everyday lives, according to 2 Thessalonians 1:3?

One of my favorite flowers in the garden is an annual called cosmos. They have very tall stems, often bringing up their blooms and wispy soft greenery more than four feet into the air. Just one plant can become a misty green bush, covered with dozens of nodding flowers. The blooms themselves come in soft pink, lavender, magenta, and fuchsia, each with a small yellow center—like daisies. The first few years I put them into my own garden, I was tremendously disappointed. They grew, but the plants were tall and spindly, often having only one or two flowers at the top. One of these plants, standing alone, was quickly blown over by the wind. They looked pitiful. What had I done wrong?

I had never known that my precious plants needed pinching. While a young plant is just starting out, a gardener must come along and nip the top right off the plant. In response, the plant sends out two new branches to grow upwards from the broken spot. In a few weeks, the gardener comes again, pinching those new stems, and again new branches fan out to take their place. By this prudent and purposeful pruning, the cosmos become dense, bushy plants that bloom well into the fall. It's even better if you plant a lot of cosmos together in a clump, because as the plants grow up and branch out together, they help to hold each other up!

Sometimes God has to do a little pruning in our lives. There are things we must let go. There are events that force us to branch out in unexpected ways. Even when these changes pinch a little, God's purpose is for our good—strength and beauty in our souls. And when we are all growing together, we can support those around us, even as they are helping us to stand.

7. A vital part of encouraging growth is confronting the things that stunt growth. In our spiritual lives, that means confronting sin. What does Galatians 6:7, 8 tell us about what we plant and what we harvest?

> *I can tell you from experience that I honestly don't know where I would be today if my friends hadn't loved me enough to point out inappropriate things in me that needed attention. If we're not willing to rely on the love, honesty, and caring of our friends and loved ones to "sharpen" us, we'll wind up a menace to the rest of the human race.*
>
> Luci Swindoll

8. When it comes to sin in young lives, my mother–in–law has a favorite saying. "You've got to nip it in the bud." How do we take care of sin, according to 1 John 1:9? And what should our attitude be towards that sin according to John 5:14?

> *Encouragement doesn't have to be profound...It just needs to be expressed.*
>
> Barbara Johnson

9. What kind of growth does Paul encourage in 1 Thessalonians 4:1?

✦ DIGGING DEEPER ✦

This week, take some extra time to read this passage from Ephesians. Then turn it into a Scripture prayer, personalizing it and applying its truths to your own heart and life.

He Himself gave some to be apostles, some prophets, some evangelists, and some pastors and teachers, for the equipping of the saints for the work of ministry, for the edifying of the body of Christ, till we all come to the unity of the faith and of the knowledge of the Son of God, to a perfect man, to the measure of the stature of the fullness of Christ; that we should no longer be children, tossed to and fro and carried about with every wind of doctrine, by the trickery of men, in the cunning craftiness of deceitful plotting, but, speaking the truth in love, may grow up in all things into Him who is the head—Christ—from whom the whole body, joined and knit together by what every joint supplies, according to the effective working by which every part does its share, causes growth of the body for the edifying of itself in love. —Ephesians 4:11–16

✦ PONDER & PRAY ✦

This week, pray for growth. Ask the LORD to help you pursue Him in paths that will lead to your good and His glory. Pray that He will open your eyes to the things slowing you down—stunting your spiritual growth. He can give you a teachable heart, and He is very willing to give you encouragement as you face changes along the way. Make it your desire to grow in grace, and in the knowledge of Jesus, your LORD.

✦ TRINKETS TO TREASURE ✦

Your gift for this week is a smiling reminder to keep following after God. He scatters encouragement in front of you just like kernels of corn before a flock of hens; so accept a few kernels of corn as your reminder. God is leading you along, urging you forward, and helping you grow. Watch for His encouragement as you pursue His ways.

✦ Notes & Prayer Requests ✦

CHAPTER 5

IT'S A GIFT!

"AS EACH ONE HAS RECEIVED A GIFT,
MINISTER IT TO ONE ANOTHER, AS GOOD STEWARDS
OF THE MANIFOLD GRACE OF GOD."

1 Peter 4:10

ome people are so hard to shop for. These are the folks that either have everything or need nothing. But then there are those people who are hard to receive gifts *from*. They have a knack for giving the most baffling gifts—gifts that make you wonder, *what were they thinking?* Or else, *what must they think of me?* Personally, I prefer an item be either practical or pretty. Best yet is the object with both qualities. Unfortunately, many things that come our way are neither. So, we dedicate a closet shelf to life's accumulation of oddities, or we hold a garage sale. Who wants to hang on to a gift they cannot put to good use?

God gives us gifts. His gifts are personalized, tailor–made, and exceedingly useable.

CLEARING + THE + COBWEBS

What would you say
was the most unusual
or useless gift
you've ever
received?

What's more, He expects us to put our gifts to good use within the Church. What gifts has your Heavenly Father bestowed upon you? Are you using them?

1. Paul lets us know "there are diversities of gifts" (1 Cor. 12:4). Did you know encouragement is a spiritual gift? Take a look at what the first part of Romans 12:8 says.

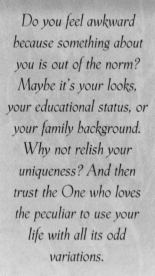

Do you feel awkward because something about you is out of the norm? Maybe it's your looks, your educational status, or your family background. Why not relish your uniqueness? And then trust the One who loves the peculiar to use your life with all its odd variations.

Patsy Clairmont

2. What should our attitude towards the spiritual gifts be? Paul tells us in 1 Corinthians 12:31.

3. We should not want spiritual gifts in order to possess them, or to complete our collection, or boast of our gains. They are given for a purpose, according to 1 Corinthians 14:12. What is that?

4. Peter insists we be good stewards of God's gifts. What does he tell us to do in 1 Peter 4:10?

5. Paul urged Timothy not to "neglect the gift that is in you" (1 Tim. 4:14). In fact, he later urged Timothy to remember the gifts God had given them, and to do what? It's in 2 Timothy 1:6.

> *When we try to do and act like other people, we are acting in an unauthorized capacity. When we try to be someone we're not, when we try to emulate gifts, skills, and characteristics that are not ours, we abuse the authority we have been given as individuals whom God has blessed with a unique purpose.*
>
> Thelma Wells

My Mother has the gift of encouragement. When I was a girl, she belonged to a TOPS® group—Take Off Pounds Sensibly®. The neighborhood ladies met every Tuesday morning at the community center, weighed in, swapped low–cal recipes, encouraged each other to hang in there, and then went out to lunch together. It was the social event of the week! Well, my Mom decided these ladies needed to have their lives spiced up a little bit. Just for fun, she started sending anonymous cards. She'd find funny cards, recycle used cards, or make a silly card, then send it off in the mail signed, *The TOPS Phantom*. It didn't take long for the buzz to get started. Nobody could figure out who the Phantom was—even my Mom "received" cards to show everyone. After months of fun, Mom decided to end the ruse. So for Halloween, she decided to arrive at the Tuesday morning meeting dressed as the Phantom. She donned tights and a black leotard, and made herself a cape with TP sewn onto it. She put white paint all over her face, outlined her eyes with black, and put a black ski cap over her hair. I still have a picture of her! The local ladies were dumbfounded when my Mom walked into the meeting, and nobody recognized her until she started laughing! Sometimes you have to be willing to give it your all in order to encourage those around you. Good one, Mom!

6. Who is the most famous encourager in the Bible? He's first mentioned in Acts 4:36.

You might appear to be different—or even strange—to some people. But remember, God made you in his image for his glory. Use your uniqueness to edify people and glorify God.

Thelma Wells

7. What else do we discover about this great encourager in Acts 11:24? List some of his admirable qualities.

✦ Notes & Prayer Requests ✦

✦ Notes & Prayer Requests ✦

CHAPTER 6

YOUR EXPERIENCE CAN ENCOURAGE OTHERS

"I AM SENDING HIM TO YOU FOR THIS REASON—
SO THAT YOU WILL KNOW HOW WE ARE, AND HE CAN
ENCOURAGE YOU."

Ephesians 6:22 NCV

So many young women believe they are the only ones who have whatever particular problem they may be facing. A young mother might look at another woman who seems to have it all together. She may seem happily married, peaceful, confident, and joyful. Her kids are neat and respectful, have whole chapters of Scripture memorized, and always wear matching socks. Meanwhile, the young mother can barely get the family out the door on Sunday mornings, struggles with a colicky baby and a two–year–old who bites, and is teetering somewhere

CLEARING + THE + COBWEBS

Of all the people you know, whom do you most enjoy getting news from?

between depression and hysteria. This poor, young lady feels overwhelmed, frustrated, panicky, and desperate—and all she needs to know is that she is not alone. All she would need is for an older, wiser woman to come alongside her and let her know: "I've been through what you're going through now. Hang in there. It'll be okay. What I am now is a culmination of all of my life thus far. It didn't happen overnight. What's more, what I am now is not the pinnacle of my life, for God is still working in my heart. God is working in your life too!"

We should not try to hide all the bumps we've hit along life's road. We've all had embarrassing moments. We've all made mistakes. God doesn't want us to hide our failures from the world so we come off looking good. He wants us to learn from those struggles, and then use them to encourage those around us. In this way, our stories become less about us, and more about how God has proved faithful.

1. Personal reflection—telling others about how God has touched our hearts and taught us lessons—is an effective tool for encouraging the faith of others. What invitation was given during a service in Acts 13:15?

2. Sometimes we need to be willing to go out of our way to give encouragement—to stop what we're doing or what we'd planned to do in order to be there for someone. Take a look at a couple of examples of Paul taking time to encourage others in Acts 16:40 and Acts 20:1.

3. Paul knew the value of encouragement. He was always sending emissaries back to the churches he'd planted. Who did Paul send out in Ephesians 6:21, 22 and in Colossians 4:7–9? Why were they sent?

4. Even Paul planned trips into his schedule that would refresh and encourage his own faith. What does he write in Romans 15:32?

5. In all the trips Paul and his friends took, what made them such a source of encouragement? Why were these visits so valuable?

> *Vital life lessons cannot be learned in obscurity and isolation. They are learned in community as we are forced to face ourselves as we really are and love enough to want to change.*
>
> Sheila Walsh

arly on in our married lives, my husband and I attended a little church pastured by my husband's brother. He preached the Word, and his wife played the piano. When the news came that we would soon be an Uncle and Aunt, we were thrilled. In fact, the whole congregation was thrilled. But then, barely before we had gotten used to the idea that a baby was on the way, there was a miscarriage. It was awful and sad. In our sorrow, we couldn't think of a thing to say. But God didn't need us to say a thing. As soon as word reached our little congregation, we surrounded our pastor and his wife with love and prayers. And what's more, women who had experienced miscarriages started coming out of the woodwork! They spoke up, shared their own stories, listened with complete understanding, and encouraged the aching heart of their sister in Christ.

This day, LORD, thank you for the believers in my life who have testified to your goodness. Show me how to bring to others the blessings I have received from these dear brothers and sisters in Christ. Amen.

Thelma Wells

6. Communication is essential for encouragement to occur. We have to talk about God's hand in our lives and our experiences. Paul's heart was lifted every time he received news from his fellow believers. What brought him joy in the letter he received from the church in Corinth? His response is in 2 Corinthians 7:7.

7. Encouragement goes both ways. When someone has given you a needed lift, letting them know God has been using them in your life will be an encouragement to them! Paul mentions this in 1 Corinthians 16:18. How are we to treat our encouragers?

8. Your testimony of God's faithfulness may be all a person needs to give them the determination to persevere through the trials they are facing right now. What were Paul's circumstances when he received encouragement from the church in Thessalonica? Did he resent the fact that they were flourishing?

> *I am committed to community. It is the church, it is our calling, but it is only as we are real with God and broken before him that we have anything to bring to one another.*
>
> Sheila Walsh

9. Paul's many benedictions are precious to me. Read his final messages to the people he held close to his heart in 2 Corinthians 13:11. What did he ask of them?

✦ DIGGING DEEPER ✦

Sharing doesn't come easily to us. It's the first good behavior our parents try to coax out of us. God asks us to share freely of our resources and possessions to help other believers when they are in need. Have you ever considered that sharing words of encouragement and testimonies of God's power in your life would also be welcome gifts to others? Take a look at these verses, which all talk about having a willingness to share.

- 2 Corinthians 9:13
- Philemon 1:6
- 1 Timothy 6:18
- Hebrews 13:16

✦ PONDER & PRAY ✦

Have you ever thought your testimony was a little boring? As you go through this week, take an introspective tour of your life. How has God been leading you along? Where can you see His hand carrying you through? What stories could you tell that might encourage the faith of someone else? Pray for God to give you opportunities to encourage others with your testimony—the testimony of God's love and power.

✦ TRINKETS TO TREASURE ✦

Your gift for this week is the heart and hand design. It's a simple pattern often used in Shaker and Amish societies. Its message is "Hands to work, hearts to God." In the dictionary, "heart and hand" is said to mean enthusiastic cooperation. So your own heart and hand trinket this week can serve to remind you that when you give your heart to God, and enthusiastically cooperate with His plans for your life, He will be able to use you to do His work. This may include opening your heart to someone in need of encouragement, and telling about how God has had a hand in your past.

✦ NOTES & PRAYER REQUESTS ✦

CHAPTER 7

LOVE ONE ANOTHER

"A NEW COMMANDMENT I GIVE TO YOU,
THAT YOU LOVE ONE ANOTHER; AS I HAVE LOVED YOU,
THAT YOU ALSO LOVE ONE ANOTHER."

John 13:34

The year the new VW Bug® came out, my mother–in–law bought one. Aren't they just the cutest little cars? Hers is black, and she keeps the little bud vase in the dashboard stocked with a spray of pink roses—her signature flower. She named her car Sophia. My children all know that Grandma drives a black bug, and even a one–year–old can distinguish a VW Beetle® from the other cars in traffic. Everywhere we go, from freeways to back ways, the kids pick them out—red ones, yellow ones, blue ones, and lime green ones. And invariably they will sing out "I see a Bug! Is it Grandma?"

Jesus told us that, because of our love for others, we would be easy to pick out in this world—just like VW Bug® is easy to

CLEARING
✦ THE ✦
COBWEBS

If you could choose any kind of car to drive, what car would perfectly suit your personality, and why?

spot on the freeway. We'll stand out because we're different. "By this all will know that you are My disciples, if you have love for one another" (John 13:35). Do you stand out from the crowd?

1. John said, "If God so loved us, we also ought to love one another" (1 John 4:11). Where does the ability to love one another come from, according to 1 Thessalonians 3:12?

> We are the body of Christ, and deep within each of us is a thirst to be known and loved, to be part of the stream of life. As we sing the psalms together, we see ourselves and each other, and yet we see our frailties within the context of the grace and mercy of God.
>
> Sheila Walsh

2. How do we know how to be loving, according to 1 Thessalonians 4:9?

3. Love for one another isn't optional. Throughout the books written by John, the beloved disciple, we find reference after reference that love is a must!

• What does Jesus say about our love for one another in John 15:17?

• What does God the Father demand, according to 1 John 3:23?

• How long have Christians known about Christ's expectation of love, according to 1 John 3:11 and 2 John 1:5?

• According to 1 John 4:7, 8, what is God, and what is the characteristic of a woman who truly knows God?

4. Why should we always be loving towards one another, according to Romans 12:5?

> *I used to think that I could carry a few of my more wounded sisters over the finishing line, but I realize now what a disservice that is. It is not love. We are not called to take each other's burdens away; we are called to share that burden, to walk alongside. We are called to encourage one another to keep our eyes on Jesus, the author and finisher of our faith.*
>
> Sheila Walsh

5. How does love play itself out? In other words, how do we treat someone with love? How does Paul describe this attitude in Ephesians 4:2?

*Y*ou could probably name all kinds of little things the people closest to you do. You know—little habits nobody else would notice. But because you're around them so much, you've picked up on them and know them well. Often, they don't even realize they're doing these things—the habits are so engrained. These quirks in our personalities are often what makes us *us*! Yet too often, we let the idiosyncrasies of those we love drive us crazy. This is when Paul's words in Ephesians 4:2 come in most handy. The little phrase at the end of the verse, "bearing with one another in love," is just a nice way of saying we will put up with one another's oddities for the sake of our love for them.

6. Why does Peter say we should hang on to a fervent love for each other in 1 Peter 4:8?

7. How are we supposed to love each other, according to John 15:12?

> As far back as I can remember, Mother had friends and was constantly inviting them to dinner or parties at our house, to meet at church, come over for coffee, play forty-two, go shopping, or (on occasion) come with us on family vacations. Whatever...she was gathering up folks who wanted or needed companionship, and she genuinely enjoyed their company. Her heart and her life were rich with meaningful friendships. In that respect, I wanted to be like her.
>
> Luci Swindoll

8. How do we show our love for one another, according to Romans 12:10?

9. How are we supposed to love one another according to 1 Peter 1:22?

> *I've learned that when we open our hands, our arms, our hearts, and let freedom ring, those we love will want to be with us—because we don't demand it of them.*
>
> Luci Swindoll

10. We often feel God's love most clearly when those around us show it to us. How does John explain this phenomenon in 1 John 4:12?

✦ DIGGING DEEPER ✦

Encouragement stems from our love for one another. It is one of the ways we express love. In order to dig deeper this week, take a few minutes to carefully consider this passage from 1 John. Go through it phrase–by–phrase until you understand it completely, and then personalize it by turning it into a prayer from your own heart.

This is how God showed his love to us: He sent his one and only Son into the world so that we could have life through him. This is what real love is: It is not our love for God; it is God's love for us in sending his Son to be the way to take away our sins. Dear friends, if God loved us that much we also should love each other.
—1 John 4:9–11 NCV

✦ PONDER & PRAY ✦

This week we have considered the fact that love is a *must* in our Christian lives. Pray this week for God to fill your heart with kind affection and brotherly love for your brothers and sisters in Christ. Then, out of love, reach out and encourage those around you, thus perfecting God's love by passing it along.

✦ TRINKETS TO TREASURE ✦

Love is for sharing, so this week's trinket is a gift that will remind you to keep the love flowing—a piece of pipe. Sure, they're good for fixing sinks and stuff, but this little beauty will be your reminder that if you try to keep all the love God shares with you to yourself, you'll end up all clogged up! Don't be stingy. Find ways to keep love flowing to those around you. It will encourage their hearts, and it will encourage your faith.

✦ NOTES & PRAYER REQUESTS ✦

✦ Notes & Prayer Requests ✦

CHAPTER 8

"ONE ANOTHER" ATTITUDES

"COMFORT EACH OTHER AND EDIFY ONE ANOTHER,
JUST AS YOU ALSO ARE DOING."

1 Thessalonians 5:11

Do you know someone whose home is the picture of familial bliss? Their children all get along together—encouraging one another, serving one another, helping one another. They understand the differences in their personalities and the ways God has gifted them. They never get jealous of each other. They rejoice when something good happens to someone else in their family. They share in the tears and comfort those who are hurting. They aren't concerned with outdoing one another, because they know that, as a part of the same family, they share in every blessing and joy.

Okay, don't laugh—or cry. Perhaps in a world without sin, all families might be

CLEARING ✦ THE ✦ COBWEBS

When you were young, did you have one very special toy you didn't share with anyone else? What was that?

like this. But reality finds folks dealing with children who are selfish and manipulative. They truly believe they are the center of the universe, and all the rest of the family's lives should revolve around their wishes. Their only spiritual gift seems to be knowing what will make their sister burst into tears. They are not failures when bickering and teasing and sibling rivalries crop up in their homes. They're just witnessing the effects of sin on the human condition in a very up–close and personal way. We can only pray for God's help in wisely guiding growing youngsters.

Just like anywhere else, relationships in the body of Christ experience the strain of sin. Within the Church, we all share the same Father, so we are spiritual siblings, all in need of maturing. We face the same kinds of problems in this community as we do in our homes. We tend to act selfishly, get our feelings hurt, say cutting things, and withhold encouragement. Let's take a look at what the New Testament says about our relationships with one another.

Heavenly Father, Create within our hearts a broader, more kindly inclination to extend our hand to whomever You send along this slippery path of life. May we lovingly hold each other up and keep each other from falling. Inspire and enable us to "be there" for each other as You are there for each of us.

Marilyn Meberg

1. How many "one anothers" can you think of? Whose life does yours touch on a regular basis?

2. What do Romans 12:16 and Romans 15:5 say our attitude towards one another should be?

3. Believers shouldn't play favorites in the Church. How does Paul say we should care for one another in 1 Corinthians 12:25?

4. Ephesians 4:32 gives us a few different "one another" attitudes we should use in caring and encouraging one another. What are they?

5. First Peter 4:9 gives us a one another attitude to have, but it comes with a condition. This must have been a lesson that needed learning, because James says the very same thing in James 5:9. What is it?

> So often these days we hide within the walls of large churches. We come in as strangers and we leave the same way. We smile at one another, give the impression that we are the one family that has it all together, and go home to our private wars. Life was not meant to be that cold. Respectability is a thin coat on a cold day. It is better to be known with all our hypocrisy and failings.
>
> Sheila Walsh

$\mathcal{T}$here is no better picture of a "one another" attitude than the one you find in a Sunday morning classroom full of two–year–olds. They have a definite sense of equality. It's all for one and one for all! In other words, if one child has a sipper cup of juice, they would all like juice. If the animal crackers come out, they all expect to receive their handful. And if one little guy gets left out, someone will pipe up to let the teacher know about it.

Are you making sure your sisters are getting their fair share of love and encouragement this week?

6. What attitude does Romans 14:13 say we should not carry against our brothers and sisters in Christ?

As much as we conceal and cover up, women long to be uncovered, discovered and known. As much as we run and hide, we have a far deeper longing to be found.

Nicole Johnson

7. What "one another" do we find in Mark 9:50?

8. What attitude should we have towards one another, according to Ephesians 5:21 and 1 Peter 5:5?

9. Lastly, how does Paul say we should treat one another in Colossians 3:13?

✦ DIGGING DEEPER ✦

When I was in the fifth grade, my teacher made our class memorize nearly all of Romans 12. I still have most of the bits and pieces lodged in my heart, though I'm not sure I could still string them together for a proper quoting of the passage. This week, for digging deeper, read through Romans 12:9–21 and make a list of all the ways in which we can present a godly attitude towards one another.

✦ PONDER & PRAY ✦

In so much of our devotional life, we focus on strengthening our personal relationship with God. Sometimes, we neglect the building of our relationships with each other. That might mean getting outside of our comfort zones. This week pray for God to help you reach outward. Ask Him to help us treat other people in the same way He has treated us. When showing love and kindness does not come easily, pray for His help and inspiration.

✦ TRINKETS TO TREASURE ✦

In the body of Christ, our attitude towards one another should be "All for one and one for all!" With that motto in mind, your gift today is a Three Musketeers® candy bar. (You'll remember this was their rallying call as well.) In our case, the "all for One" is all for Christ. We each belong to Jesus, and we give our all for Him. The "One for all" is a reminder that God is for us, and He loves each of us equally. So don't fall into family squabbling, but instead join forces with all believers. It's a great way to encourage each other!

✦ NOTES & PRAYER REQUESTS ✦

CHAPTER 9

"ONE ANOTHER" ACTIONS

"THROUGH LOVE SERVE ONE ANOTHER."

Galatians 5:13

"One another" is a theme that runs throughout the New Testament. There are so many "one another" verses, we're taking two weeks to cover them all.

So often in our devotional lives, we focus all of our attention on building our relationship with God. We read the Scriptures—studying, highlighting, underlining, and outlining. We select portions of the Bible to memorize, sticking little note cards up on the bathroom mirror and on our computer screens. We fill our hearts and minds with songs of worship and praise. We pray for God's will to be worked out in our lives, for the needs of our families, and for the furtherance of His kingdom. We buy books that will help to strengthen our

CLEARING ✦ THE ✦ COBWEBS

What is your least favorite housekeeping task?

relationship with God. We attend conferences so we can become more knowledgeable, more effective, and more zealous. With all our heart, we pursue our LORD. And that is all very good, of course.

The LORD created us with an emotional and relational need for human contact. Nothing can hearten like the hug from a caring person.

Patsy Clairmont

But one of the things God is asking us to do is open up our eyes to the people around us. We are not God's only child. We belong to a large and growing family, which spreads across the whole world. Sometimes it takes a little gentle persuasion to take off our blinders and come out of our prayer closets to see the needs of those around us. Jesus is in heaven now, so He cannot walk among us to touch those who are hurting or in need of encouragement. Instead, He asks us to be His hands and His feet. We are His means of reaching out. God works through us to lift the spirits of those around us.

1. This chapter focuses on the things we are asked to do for one another. Let's begin in Galatians 6:2. What does Paul request of us?

2. What does Paul encourage us to do in Ephesians 4:25 and Colossians 3:9?

3. What reasons does each of the verses above give for being truthful with one another?

4. What does Paul ask us to do for one another in Romans 15:7?

5. What does Jesus ask us to do in John 13:14?

How are you? Are you pining for the fellowship that surpasses all others? Get yourself to the nearest Christian and connect. Spend time with fellow believers rejoicing over what you have in Jesus. Sing some songs. Laugh together. Pray for one another. Hug each other. Celebrate the blessed tie that binds you to one another in Christian love.

Marilyn Meberg

From time to time, we give in to the fact that it's time to do a little spring cleaning. With a wide range of cleaning supplies, we tackle the dirt and grime that finds its way into our homes. Scouring sinks, changing bedding, doing dishes, loading the washing machine, mopping floors, dusting furniture, polishing windows, and shaking out rugs. It wouldn't be so bad if we had a little help! At some point, we want to throw down our dustpan and throw up our hands, and cry out, "I'm not the cleaning woman, you know!" We sometimes feel like slaves to our tasks.

But aren't we? Jesus was willing to do a slave's job by washing His disciples' feet. And when He was done, He told His disciples they should serve one another too. Jesus didn't say we would always be appreciated. He didn't say we'd never be taken for granted. What He asks of us is to love and to serve. What better place to practice than in our own home.

> This is the heartbeat of celebrating friendship. Rejoicing, honoring, applauding, commending, saluting, toasting the wonderful people in our lives. Not for what they do, but for who they are, and for what they mean to us.
>
> Nicole Johnson

6. What are we called to do in Galatians 5:13?

7. What kinds of behavior does James urge us to avoid with one another?

8. There are a couple of other "don'ts" in Galatians 5:26 when it comes to one anothers. What are they?

9. Take a look at this series of verses. Our mouths should not be used to cut down fellow believers, but to build them up and encourage them. Each of these verses talks about this:

- What does Romans 15:14 say we, who are full of goodness and knowledge, should be able to do?

- How does Ephesians 5:19 say we should speak to one another?

- What is the source of all these good things that flow from our mouths, according to Colossians 3:16?

✦ DIGGING DEEPER ✦

Just as encouragement flows out of our love for each other, service is an outpouring of love. We are able to serve cheerfully when the love that inspires the service is from God. Let's dig a little deeper, and search out just a few more verses that talk about serving one another.

- Matthew 20:28
- 1 Timothy 6:2
- Colossians 3:24

✦ PONDER & PRAY ✦

If you want to encourage one another, you start with God and love. Sharing this love with others is the greatest source of encouragement available. We share God's love with other believers and with one another. This week, as you pray, ask God to show you ways to encourage the "one anothers" in your life, even if it means being willing to serve them. In this way, we follow after Jesus.

✦ TRINKETS TO TREASURE ✦

Your trinket to treasure this week is a little gift to help you remember Jesus' call to serve—a nice soft cloth for dusting. Whether you're wiping up a messy spill or helping to wipe away the tears from someone's eyes, you are prepared. And in your service, you will bring encouragement to many hearts.

✦ Notes & Prayer Requests ✦

✦ Notes & Prayer Requests ✦

CHAPTER 10

WHERE IT'S NEEDED MOST

"STRENGTHEN THOSE WHO HAVE TIRED HANDS, AND
ENCOURAGE THOSE WHO HAVE WEAK KNEES."

Isaiah 35:3 NLT

*I*n ancient mythology, there is the story of a woman whose life was beset with hardships—some we can probably relate to. This gal was a newlywed, but she wasn't having much of a honeymoon. Her mother–in–law didn't approve of her (she wasn't her son's equal). She suspected her husband was hiding things from her, and suspicion robbed her of any happiness. Her sisters were jealous of her wealthy new husband, and were doing their best to drive a wedge between the couple. All of this subterfuge managed to thrust the couple apart, but the woman wanted to reconcile. As was the way in most ancient myths, the only way to mend the broken relationship was through the

CLEARING ✦ THE ✦ COBWEBS

If you were having a really bad day, what one thing would help turn things around for you and encourage you?

accomplishment of several impossible tasks. For the sake of love, our heroine submitted to tests that were meant to prove her worthiness. The first test found our weary woman seated on a stool in front of a mountain of grain made of wheat, rye, sesame, oats, millet, flax, and rice—all mixed together like a huge hill of birdseed. She was told she must separate all the grains, making heaps of each kind, before day's end.

Sometimes, when I begin my day, I feel like I'm facing that pile of grain. There's so much to do, and it all takes so much time. How can I possibly get it all done by day's end? The depth and breadth of my responsibilities leave me discouraged. Even if I roll up my sleeves and tackle the day with energy, there's no sign that I'm actually making any headway. Slow progress leaves me dispirited. What's the use of trying? Though a little lift is always welcome, these are the times when encouragement is needed most. We need our Savior and our friends to come alongside us. Any kindness, no matter how small, helps that pile we face to dwindle away. That's the power of encouragement.

When the floodwaters of the cesspool have come up to your very soul, you don't need challenges; you need comfort. You need a friend to come alongside and say, "I am hurting with you...I am standing with you...I am weeping with you. I am undergirding you as best I can. Link your shield of faith with mine and somehow we will make it together."

Barbara Johnson

1. Jeremiah, "the weeping prophet," spoke freely about the despair in his heart. Who was available to come alongside him in the midst of his weeping, according to Lamentations 1:16?

2. In contrast, Paul speaks of the encouragement he derived from his friends. In Acts 28:14, 15, we find Paul making his way towards Rome and a Roman trial. When the believers in that city find out he is on his way, they form a welcoming party and go out to greet him on the road. What was Paul's reaction to their presence?

3. Are we supposed to limit our encouragement to our own little Christian cliques? Look at Paul's compliment to the church in Thessalonica in Thessalonians 4:10. How far did their ministry of caring reach?

Encouragement is to a friendship what confetti is to a party. It's light, refreshing, and fun, and you always end up finding little pieces of it stuck on you later.

Nicole Johnson

4. What does our encouragement do for those around us, according to 1 Thessalonians 5:11?

5. Paul spoke often about encouragement to the church in Thessalonica. Read 1 Thessalonians 5:14 as it is translated in *The Message*:

> *Our counsel is that you warn the freeloaders to get a move on. Gently encourage the stragglers, and reach out for the exhausted, pulling them to their feet. Be patient with each person, attentive to individual needs.*

According to Paul, who needs encouragement the most? What can be done to encourage them?

*R*emember the lady from our opening illustration? I suppose you'd like to know how things worked out for her. She had been ordered to sort through a mountain of mixed grains, making neat piles of wheat, millet, rye, and oats. She wept at the enormous task set before her, but she was not as alone as she thought she was. The tiny ants heard her crying and took pity on her. With their small size and great numbers, they made short work of the grain pile. Where the young woman could not succeed alone, others came alongside and helped her through. In the end, true love triumphed over every obstacle, and the couple lived happily ever after.

Even a fairy tale can remind us of God's truth. When we are faced with difficult trials, God wants us to remember we are not as alone as we might feel. With the help, prayers, and encouragement of our friends, our discouragement melts away, just like that pile of grain.

> *As Christians one of the greatest temptations we face is to quit. As I travel and meet people all over the country I hear more tales of discouragement than of blatant sin.*
>
> Sheila Walsh

6. In Proverbs 12:25, what does wise Solomon have to say about the value of an encouraging word? What does it often offset?

7. An important aspect of encouraging someone who really needs it is using the right words. What does Ephesians 4:29 say about choosing our words?

> We come out of deep grief as different persons than we were before. We can come out stronger, kinder, and more understanding of the problems of others, or we can come out bitter and self–pitying, uninterested in others' problems because we have too many of our own.
>
> Barbara Johnson

8. Isaiah talks a bit about how a community can rally and support one another. "They encourage one another with the words, 'Be strong!'" (Is. 41:6 NLT). Let's take a look at the place Job had in his own circle of influence. How does Eliphaz describe Job's ability to encourage in Job 4:3?

9. What can a little encouragement help us to do, according to Revelation 14:12?

✦ DIGGING DEEPER ✦

Everyone needs help now and again. In fact, God thought it was such a necessity, He would not leave Adam alone. "I will make him a helper" (Gen. 2:18). In a way, we women were given the role of encourager right from the start. Without Eve, who would have been right there to tell Adam what a good job he was doing in the garden? But being a helper doesn't mean we are of secondary value—a mere sidekick. Who else was called a helper for us in the Scriptures? Take a look:

- Psalm 10:14
- Psalm 54:4
- John 15:26; 16:7
- Psalm 30:10
- John 14:16, 26
- Hebrews 13:6

✦ PONDER & PRAY ✦

Even when we are facing the worst days, most of us try to put up a brave front and paste on a smile. We may be crying inside, staggering under heavy burdens, but we don't like to tell people about them. This week, pray for God to help you see when your sister is struggling. Then you can come alongside her, pray for her, and encourage her along the way.

✦ Trinkets to Treasure ✦

This week's trinket will help you remember what to do on those days when you need encouragement the most. A tiny jar of mixed grains is hardly a mountain, but it will be enough to bring our story to mind. When it's hard to face a complicated day, even the tiniest of encouragements can help you see it through. Even a little bit of help will make that pile dwindle away.

✦ Notes & Prayer Requests ✦

_____

_____

_____

_____

_____

_____

_____

_____

_____

_____

✦ Notes & Prayer Requests ✦

CHAPTER 11

ENCOURAGING EPISTLES

"THEY GATHERED THE CHURCH AND GAVE THEM THE
LETTER. WHEN THEY READ IT, THEY WERE VERY HAPPY
BECAUSE OF THE ENCOURAGING MESSAGE."

Acts 15:30, 31 NCV

College was exciting for me. After spending my whole life in a small town and attending a small Christian academy, the college campus seemed vast. There were so many interesting things to see and do. I loved watching all the people, I loved my dorm room, I loved the new taste of freedom, and I even loved my professors. Once I got there, I never wanted to leave!

Part of the daily routine at college was a stop at the mailboxes. They were sweet, old-fashioned brass boxes with little windows on the front and a simple combination lock. Between classes, I'd peek through the window to see if anyone had been thinking of me. Most often, the box

CLEARING
✦ THE ✦
COBWEBS

How many different
mailing addresses
have you had
over the years?

was filled with flyers—upcoming sporting events, senior recitals, variety shows, fundraisers, ministry opportunities, job postings, clubs to join, and the latest edition of the campus newspaper. Most of this stuff ended up in a conveniently positioned recycling bin. But what I loved was "real mail."

Sometimes, there would be a card from Grandma in Wisconsin or a letter from my little sister that spilled all her high school adventures. The joy of joys was the little pink slip of paper that meant a package was waiting for me at the post office window. Care packages from home were filled with gifts and letters and pictures from my folks. They encouraged me to no end. Though I loved where I was, it was good to know I was loved from where I'd been.

1. It's good to be reminded that most of the books in our New Testament are epistles—letters! Our Bibles are filled with "real mail" that brought joy and encouragement to the earliest believers. What does Peter say is his purpose in writing to the church in 1 Peter 5:12?

2. John's letters are meant to encourage his fellow believers. Who is he writing to, according to 1 John 2:13?

3. The letter writers of the Bible depended upon their readers to accept their words—to hear them with teachable hearts. What is the writer's plea in Hebrews 13:22?

4. Epistles though they might be, these New Testament books were no ordinary letters. The apostles wrote "according to the authority which the LORD has given me for edification" (2 Cor. 13:10). How did Paul explain this truth in 1 Corinthians 14:37?

> When we do little acts of kindness that make life more bearable for someone else, we are walking in love as the Bible commands us. One way to do this costs only the sum of a postage stamp, a little paper, and ink. Every one of us has felt the nudge to write someone a letter or note. Many times we don't follow up on it; we tell ourselves it wouldn't matter anyway. When we think this way, we miss giving and receiving splashes of joy.
>
> Barbara Johnson

5. Paul seems to say a lot of the same things in his letter to his dear friend in Philemon 1:21. Paul knows if he asks something from his friend—even something hard—Philemon will do what?

6. Paul's letters all carry common themes. His message remained consistent. Many of the epistles were circulated amongst several different churches. Believers heard the same admonitions and challenges again and again. Was Paul worried it would get old for them?

*H*ave you opened up your mailbox with a smile lately? It's pretty hard to do. After all, what do you usually find? Shopping circulars, advertisements, coupons, approval letters from credit card companies, and bills, bills, bills! The supply of junk mail seems endless. The contents of the daily paper are far from uplifting. Everyone seems to be trying to sell you things you don't need. What wouldn't we give for a little bit of "real mail?"

What is real mail? *Not* the sort of mail that is addressed to "Mrs. Joan Smith OR Current Resident." It's a cheerful card in a brightly colored envelope. It's a hand–written letter with your own name scrawled across the envelope. It's a post-card from a faraway city that brings a smile to your face. Real mail comes in personalized envelopes—covered with interesting stamps, funny stickers, and P.S. messages that make you laugh. Real mail means someone who loves you is thinking of you. Real mail reminds you that encouragement can be passed along for the price of a postage stamp.

Postcards are one of the simplest and greatest ways in the world to capture the moment. They're colorful, easy to acquire, quick to write, and inexpensive. In a few minutes time you tell somebody on the other side of the world that you love her and are thinking of her. I write cards all the time, even from home.

Luci Swindoll

7. Still, for all their Spirit–breathed, God–given, authoritative teaching, the epistles are filled with personal little messages for dear friends. One of the messages that often came through was, "Hope to see you soon!"

- What did Paul say he was hoping for in 1 Timothy 3:14?

- What did John prefer to paper and ink in 3 John 1:13, 14?

- What did John say a face–to–face meeting would bring in 2 John 1:12?

8. What other reasons do our epistle writers give for their correspondence? Match up the reasons with the verses where they are mentioned.

___ To stir up pure minds   a. Romans 15:15

___ So our joy may be full   b. 1 Corinthians 10:11

___ So we will not sin   c. 2 Peter 3:1

___ To exhort us to contend   d. 1 John 1:4
for the faith

___ To remind us of grace   e. 1 John 2:1

___ Because we know the truth   f. 1 John 2:21

___ So we know we have   g. 1 John 5:13
eternal life

___ For our admonition   h. Jude 1:3

9. Paul was often aided by a colleague when composing his letters. As Paul dictated, a friend like Luke or Silvanus would write down his words for him. Paul never sent a letter without leaving his personal mark on it. He knew how important it was for his friends to see his large, familiar scrawl at the close of every letter. Take a look at an example of this in 2 Thessalonians 3:17. Why do you think Paul did this?

10. Read 2 Corinthians 3:1–3. To what does Paul compare those who have become Christians?

✦ DIGGING DEEPER ✦

There are things written to encourage our faith and to encourage our spiritual growth. There are letters we write to encourage each other—to lift our spirits. There are friends whose lives are like letters of recommendation—testifying to the faithfulness of God. And then, there is the writing that the LORD does in our lives—on our hearts and in our minds. Take a look at these two passages in Hebrews. According to Hebrews 8:10 and Hebrews 10:16, what does God write? Where does He write it and why?

✦ PONDER & PRAY ✦

One of the simplest and least expensive ways to reach out with encouragement to those around you is right though their mailbox. All it needs is a little effort on your part. Pray this week for the inspiration to put this into practice. Ask for the Spirit's hand in giving you the right words to say and the most creative way to present them.

✦ TRINKETS TO TREASURE ✦

Your trinket to treasure this week is something you cannot keep. It's a postage stamp, and I expect you to put it to use. In fact, get a whole book of stamps, and make it your mission to encourage your sisters right through their mailboxes! Before you know it, you'll be getting encouragement back through your own mailbox, and then you can keep the cancelled stamps as reminders of their encouraging epistles.

✦ NOTES & PRAYER REQUESTS ✦

CHAPTER 12

JUST THINK!

"THINK OF WAYS TO ENCOURAGE ONE ANOTHER TO OUTBURSTS OF LOVE AND GOOD DEEDS."

Hebrews 10:24 NLT

When we lived in the country, it was hard to find the little dirt road we lived on. Grosvenor was discreetly situated between two corn fields, and the street sign was set so far back from the highway most people flew by without even noticing the road existed. After dark, even those of us who lived on Grosvenor had a hard time finding it. That's because the little reflector the highway department had placed at the intersection had been hit by a snowplow the winter before. It was bent sideways, and no longer caught the light from oncoming headlights. Without that little white circle flashing in the darkness, I was sometimes forced to hit the brakes hard in order to make the turn in time.

CLEARING
✦ THE ✦
COBWEBS

Would you rather have one big gift or a steady supply of small, loving gestures throughout the year?

The first time my folks made the long trip to visit us in our new home, I tried to explain the obscurity of our little road. I gave landmarks, exact distances, and general descriptions—apologizing that we weren't easier to find. Sure enough, they overshot the turn before spotting our road. We talked about it later, and I explained how we even missed it after dark, because of that bent reflector. A couple of days later, coming home after dusk from the grocery store, I was surprised to find the reflector back in its proper position. I mentioned it to everyone as I came in with my bags. My Dad just smiled and admitted he had pulled over the day before and taken the five minutes necessary to reposition the reflector.

From that day onward, every time I passed that gleaming reflector at the end of my road, it encouraged me. My Dad cared enough to go out of his way to do something to help me. Though the gesture was small, it left a lasting reminder of my Dad's love for me.

1. Often we hope people will be encouraged just by our very presence. After all, it takes a good amount of effort just to show up some days! What excuses do we have for avoiding a commitment to encouraging others?

2. Encouragement may take a little effort, but it's fun! In *The Message*, Hebrews 10:24 reads, "Let's see how inventive we can be in encouraging love and helping out." Women in every season of life need to be loved. Write down something you could do to encourage each of these women to "help them out." Be creative!

- A college student, far from home

- A single, working woman

- A new bride

- An expectant mother

- A mommy surrounded by preschoolers

- A working mother

- A single mom

- A mother with teenagers

- An empty–nester

- A brand new grandma

- A widow

- A terminally ill woman

- An elderly friend

- A recluse

- A nursing home resident

3. Need some ideas to get started? The steady change of seasons offers inspiration for our efforts at encouraging one another. What small gifts would lift the heart of a friend on the first day of spring, summer, autumn, and winter?

> *Taking the time to gather little pieces of love, grace, strength, and hope is worth it when you shower your friendships with them. Spiritual confetti! It is the ultimate encouragement.*
>
> Nicole Johnson

4. Is four times a year not enough for you to show encouragement? For those who wish to go beyond quarterly encouragement, there are the holidays to consider! Can you think of something fun to do or send as an encouragement on these holidays?

- Ground Hog's Day

- Valentine's Day

- St. Patrick's Day

- Easter

- May Day

- Independence Day

- Thanksgiving

- Christmas

- New Year's

5. Our family has never needed much prodding to find ways to celebrate. But sometimes we need "permission" to party. All you need is a little research. What stirrings do you feel in your creativity, knowing that...

- January is National Soup Month

- February is National Wild Bird Feeding Month

- March is National Umbrella Month

- April is National Humor Month

- May is National Salsa Month

- June is National Iced Tea Month

- July is National Hot Dog Month

- August is National Goat Cheese Month

- September is National Chicken Month

- October is National Popcorn Poppin' Month

- November is National Peanut Butter Lover's Month

- December is National Bingo's Birthday Month

6. Want even more excuses to make someone smile?

- January 11–18 is International Thank You Days

- February 9–15 is National Random Acts of Kindness Week

- March 20–27 is National Spring Fever Week

- April 4–18 is National Straw Hat Week

- May 2–8 is National Postcard Week

- June 13–19 is National Hermit Week

- November 2–8 is National Split Pea Soup Week

- December 21–27 is International Lipstick Week

And it's not just weeks! There are even special days.

• January 12 is National Clean–Off–Your–Desk Day

• February 12 is Lost Penny Day

• March 26 is National Make Up Your Own Holiday Day

• April 7 is National No Housework Day

• May 12 is National Limerick Day

• June 19 is World Sauntering Day

• July 24 is National Cousin's Day

• October 15 is National Grouch Day

• December 5 is National Bathtub Party Day

How would you get your girlfriends grinning over these little–known holidays? Share a few of your ideas here.

It doesn't take much to brighten someone's day. All that's needed is something a little out of the ordinary. I'll never forget a story my husband brought home from his choir tour in London, England. Back in our college days, he was part of a large group who traveled to sing in some of the churches and cathedrals across England, Scotland, and Wales. One morning, my husband and a couple of his friends spent some of their money at a flower vendor's cart, buying a big bouquet of roses. Then the three young men went to work, trying to give the roses away, one flower at a time, to women on the street. Several ladies thought these Americans were crazy, and refused to take the proffered flowers. But many women—a dozen women, in fact—were treated to an unexpected encouragement that day. They blushed, brightened, smiled, and were thankful, all because of the gift of a rose.

One day, as I headed out the door, I filled my pockets with Snickers® bars. I had to do some errands in town, and everywhere I went I handed out these miniature candy bars. To friends, to strangers, to salespeople, to women, to children, to men. Without exception they not only were surprised by an unexpected treat, but they all also snickered. Something about the gift caused them to pause, smile, and release a little giggle.

Patsy Clairmont

7. We encourage one another through life's little ups and downs because it is enjoyable to brighten one another's days. But there are times when someone close to us truly needs a lift. That's the time for care packages. What kinds of things would truly encourage the following people?

- A grandchild or niece who lives far away

- A college freshman

- A soldier stationed overseas

- A newcomer to your congregation

- Someone recovering from surgery

- Your Grandma, who has the blues

- An expectant mother on bed rest

- Your pastor's wife

- A missionary family

- Your mother–in–law, just because

8. What does Hebrews 10:24, 25 say we should be doing? How does this foster an encouraging atmosphere?

9. In the *New Century Version*, Hebrews 3:13 says "Encourage each other every day while it is 'today.'" Just think of what God could do through you if you took that verse to heart! Where would you start?

> *Keep looking for ways to bless others. Compete with yourself to see if you can find more creative ways to love this week than last. Brainstorm blessing projects for next year.*
>
> Barbara Johnson

✦ DIGGING DEEPER ✦

Getting along is not always an easy thing, but Paul is always urging us to hang in there with each other. One of the messages he repeats in his epistles is "Do not grow weary in doing good" (Gal. 6:9; 2 Thess. 3:13). He wants us to cooperate together because we are all a part of the body of Christ. Take a look at these three Scripture passages (and their contexts as well). They talk about our relationship within the body of Christ as being "joined" and "knit together." Why are our lives to be so interlocked?

• Ephesians 4:16

• Colossians 2:2

• Colossians 2:19

✦ PONDER & PRAY ✦

Opportunities to offer encouragement present themselves every day, but we are so busy trying to keep our own lives going we let them drift right by. Pray this week for the LORD to open your eyes to those around you and for the Spirit to inspire you with ideas for reaching out. God made us to need one another, so don't hide from your place in the Church. You are uniquely gifted to serve as an encouragement to those around you. Even if it doesn't seem like much to you, what you contribute to the family of God is something no one else can quite duplicate.

✦ TRINKETS TO TREASURE ✦

Let's close this lesson with a reminder to find little ways to encourage one another. Encouragement doesn't need to come in big, flashy, or even organized ways. A thoughtful gift, a willingness to listen, a pat on the shoulder, a cheerful attitude, a hug, a favor returned, a prayer shared, or standing together can truly be a treasure to the one who needed that little boost. The remembrance of your kindness will be like the sweet fragrance of a rose lingering in the air. So this week, your trinket is a lovely rose.

✦ Notes & Prayer Requests ✦

✦ SHALL WE REVIEW? ✦

Every chapter has added a new trinket to your treasure trove of memories. Let's remind ourselves of the lessons they hold for us!

1. A baseball.

Remember, God is always there, cheering you on. This trinket brings to mind the Host of Heaven, whose eyes are fixed on you. Can't you hear your Savior call, "Atta girl! You can do it!"

2. Trail mix.

When you hit the trails of life, you must be prepared. Knowing where to turn for nourishment and shelter is vital. This trinket will serve to remind you that the only way to remain a happy camper in your day–to–day life is by taking hold of the encouragement found in your Bible.

3. A trowel.

This is a reminder to dig a little deeper, and get past the surface chatter in your relationships. It may take a little effort to begin talking about your faith with those closest to you, but it will encourage their faith—and yours as well.

4. Kernels of corn.

This was a funny reminder to keep on following after God. He scatters encouragement in front of you just like kernels of corn before a flock of hens, so accept a few kernels of corn as a reminder of that. God is leading you along, urging you forward, and helping you grow.

5. A wooden spoon.

Whenever you see a wooden spoon, be reminded how Paul urges us to "stir up" our spiritual gifts. Don't neglect them. Don't let them gather dust on the shelves of your heart. God has given you good gifts, and He wants you to encourage others with them. So stir it up, sister!

6. Heart and hand.

This simple pattern's message is "Hands to work, hearts to God." This trinket can remind you that, when you give your heart to God and enthusiastically cooperate with His plans for your life, He will be able to use you to do His work.

7. A piece of pipe.

Love is for sharing, so this trinket reminds us to keep the love flowing. Don't be stingy, but find ways to keep love flowing to those around you. It will encourage their hearts, and it will encourage your faith.

8. A candy bar.

In the body of Christ, our attitude towards one another should be "All for one and one for all!" In our case, the "all for One" is all for Christ. We each belong to Jesus, and we give our all for Him. The "One for all" is a reminder that God is for us, and He loves each of us equally.

9. A dust cloth.

This little gift reminds us of Jesus' call to serve. Whether you're wiping up a messy spill or helping to wipe away the tears from someone's eyes, you are prepared. In your service, you will bring encouragement to many hearts.

10. Mixed grains.

A tiny jar of mixed grains is hardly a mountain, but it will be enough to bring to mind our story about the ants. When it's hard to face a complicated day, even the tiniest of encouragements can help you endure. Even a little bit of help will make that pile dwindle away.

11. A stamp.

This trinket is something you cannot keep. Make it your mission to encourage your sisters right through their mailboxes! Before you know it, you'll be receiving encouragement by return mail.

12. A rose.

This is a reminder to find little ways to encourage one another. Even a little gesture is a treasure to the one who needs a boost. The remembrance of your kindness will be like the sweet fragrance of a rose, lingering in the air.

✦ Leader's Guide ✦

Chapter 1

1. "Patience and encouragement come from God" (Rom. 15:5 NCV). The same God who is our Source of life, salvation, and strength for living, took the time to make sure we also have a ready supply of encouragement along the way. He thinks of everything!

2. "Is there any encouragement from belonging to Christ? Any comfort from his love? Any fellowship together in the Spirit?" (Phil. 2:1 NLT). What a list! Doesn't it lift your heart to realize you belong to Jesus and you are loved? You have His Spirit and you can have fellowship with other believers because you share the same Spirit.

3. "When I pray, you answer me; you encourage me by giving me the strength I need" (Ps. 138:3 NLT). David's thanks are twofold. First of all, God encourages him by answering his prayers. Secondly, David is encouraged because God gives him the strength he needs to face each day.

4. "These two things cannot change: God cannot lie when he makes a promise, and he cannot lie when he makes an oath. These things encourage us who came to God for safety. They give us strength to hold on to the hope we have been given" (Heb. 6:18 NCV). We know God doesn't lie to us, so we can take great encouragement from His promises, because we know they will come to pass.

5. "You have forgotten the encouraging words that call you his children: "My child, don't think the LORD's discipline is worth nothing, and don't stop trying when he corrects you" (Heb. 12:5 NCV). Even the discipline we receive from God can be a source of encouragement, because it means God loves us and will not leave us a prisoner to sin. "For whom the LORD loves He chastens" (Heb. 12:6).

6. "So when we are weighed down with troubles, it is for your benefit and salvation! For when God comforts us, it is so that we, in turn, can be an encouragement to you. Then you can patiently endure the same things we suffer" (2 Cor. 1:6 NLT). We can reach out and encourage those who are going through the same things we have. The same God who was faithful in carrying us through will be able to carry them.

7. Romans 15:5 says, "May God, who gives this patience and encouragement, help you live in complete harmony with each other—each with the attitude of Christ Jesus toward the other."(NLT) We are to have the same attitude towards others that Jesus would have towards us.

8. "Let nothing be done through selfish ambition or conceit, but in lowliness of mind let each esteem others better than himself. Let each of you look out not only for his own interests, but also for the interests of others. Let this mind be in you which was also in Christ Jesus…He humbled Himself and became obedient" (Phil. 2:3–5, 8). Jesus' attitude is summed up here as being one of unselfishness, consideration, humility, and obedience. You should not be "interested only in your own life, but be interested in the lives of others" (Phil. 2:4 NCV).

9. "May our LORD Jesus Christ himself and God our Father encourage you and strengthen you in every good thing you do and say. God loved us, and through his grace he gave us a good hope and encouragement that continues forever" (2 Thess. 2:17 NCV). The encouragement that God bestows will strengthen us in this life and continue for eternity.

Chapter 2

1. "Encourage me by your word" (Ps. 119:28 NLT). If you have a Bible, you hold the greatest source of encouragement you could ever hope to find.

2. "These are written that you may believe that Jesus is the Christ, the Son of God, and that believing you may have life in His name" (John 20:31). "These things I have written to you who believe in the name of the Son of God, that you may know that you have eternal life, and that you may continue to believe in the name of the Son of God" (1 John 5:13). The Bible isn't just God's scrapbook—it's written with a purpose in mind. Just like John says, these Words have been recorded so we could read them, believe them, and find life. Isn't it encouraging to know God had you in mind when He set John to writing?

3. "Such things were written in the Scriptures long ago to teach us. They give us hope and encouragement as we wait patiently for God's promises" (Rom. 15:4 NLT). The Bible gives us hope. The Bible gives us encouragement while we wait for everything to come to pass.

4. "Until I get there, focus on reading the Scriptures to the church, encouraging the believers, and teaching them" (1 Tim. 4:13 NLT). You can't keep a church going and growing just by establishing a good Secret Sister program. Fun things do lift our hearts for a time, but real encouragement does not come apart from God. Timothy was instructed to encourage the believers by reading them the Scriptures and teaching them what the truths meant for their lives. Preach it, brother!

5. "After the law of Moses and the writings of the prophets were read, the leaders of the synagogue sent a message to Paul and Barnabas: 'Brothers, if you have any message that will encourage the people, please speak'" (Acts 13:15 NCV). God's Word is a source of encouragement in and of itself, but there are times when men of God are able to help us understand the Word better and to apply the truths to our lives. Can anybody say "sermon"?

6. "Teach me, and I will hold my tongue; Cause me to understand wherein I have erred" (Job 6:24). There are times when we need to bite our tongues, keep from getting defensive or making excuses, and listen to the conviction the Word brings.

7. "Keep me from looking at worthless things. Let me live by Your Word" (Ps. 119:37 NCV). Compared to the good teaching we find in our Bibles, everything else we might turn to is worthless.

8. "We also are men with the same nature as you, and preach to you that you should turn from these useless things to the living God, who made the heaven, the earth, the sea, and all things that are in them" (Acts 14:15).

9. "Preach the word! Be ready in season and out of season. Convince, rebuke, exhort, with all longsuffering and teaching" (2 Tim. 4:2). The Word teaches, instructs, challenges, warns, urges, convinces, reproves, rebukes, exhorts, corrects, and encourages.

Chapter 3

1. Pastors, Bible study teachers, the women in our prayer groups, mentors, deaconesses, Christian friends, moms, mothers-in-law, sisters, aunts, Christian authors, songwriters, conference speakers—who enrich our lives by encouraging our faith in God.

2. "And sent Timothy, our brother and minister of God, and our fellow laborer in the gospel of Christ, to establish you and encourage you concerning your faith" (1 Thess. 3:2). Our Christian leaders are laboring for the sake of Jesus—giving their whole attention to proclaiming the gospel. They bend their efforts to establish our faith, and encourage us in it.

3. "Then Judas and Silas, both being prophets, spoke extensively to the Christians, encouraging and strengthening their faith" (Acts 15:32 NLT). By speaking God's Word to the people, these men encouraged the believers and strengthened their faith.

4. "You must teach these things and encourage your people to do them, correcting them when necessary. You have the authority to do this, so don't let anyone ignore you or disregard what you say" (Titus 2:15 NLT). Our pastors encourage us to follow the truth and live it out. Have you disregarded their messages or ignored their sermons? If so, it may be contributing to the discouragement you are facing in your life right now!

5. "He must have a strong and steadfast belief in the trustworthy message he was taught; then he will be able to encourage others with right teaching and show those who oppose it where they are wrong" (Titus 1:9 NLT). Look at these descriptions: strong, steadfast, trustworthy, and able to encourage. What's more, look at what that encouragement involves—right teaching and defending the truth of God's Word. This takes a dedication to knowing and understanding your Bible, and some practice in putting your beliefs into words.

6. "Let us not neglect our meeting together, as some people do, but encourage and warn each other, especially now that the day of his coming back again is drawing near" (Heb. 10:25 NLT). How can we be encouraged by the speaking of God's Word if we don't have a church family? How can we encourage our brothers and sisters in Christ if we do not spend time with them? Being an active member in our local church congregation is a vital part of the encouragement of our faith.

7. "Even so the LORD has commanded that those who preach the gospel should live from the gospel"(1 Cor. 9:14). What a nice, biblical way of saying, "Practice what you preach."

8. "I didn't skimp or trim in any way. Every truth and encouragement that could have made a difference to you, you got. I taught you out in public and I taught you in your homes" (Acts 20:20 MSG). Don't be selfish. Don't hold back. Give it your all. Besides, it will come back to you.

9. "I'm eager to encourage you in your faith, but I also want to be encouraged by yours. In this way, each of us will be a blessing to the other" (Rom. 1:12 NLT). Line up your attitude with Paul's, and look for ways to encourage those around you with eagerness!

Chapter 4

1. Romans 14:19 says, "pursue the things which make for peace and the things by which one may edify another." First Corinthians 14:1 urges us to pursue love and desire spiritual gifts, which are also used in encouraging one another in the church. In 1 Thessalonians 5:15, Paul says that we should "always pursue what is good both for yourselves and for all." First Timothy 6:11 finds Paul urging his spiritual son to pursue righteousness, godliness, faith, love, patience, and gentleness. Hebrews 12:14 commands us to "pursue peace with all people, and holiness." Why? Because without these things, no one will see the LORD.

2. "The church everywhere in Judea, Galilee, and Samaria had a time of peace and became stronger. Respecting the LORD by the way they lived, and being encouraged by the Holy Spirit, the group of believers continued to grow" (Acts 9:31 NCV). The Holy Spirit teaches us.

3. Paul says, "We encouraged you, we urged you, and we insisted that you live good lives for God" (1 Thess. 2:12 NCV). In *The Message*, this verse is translated to include "holding your hand, whispering encouragement, showing you step–by–step how to live well before God."

4. "As newborn babes, desire the pure milk of the word, that you may grow thereby" (1 Pet. 2:2). You cannot grow spiritually if you are not feeding yourself by reading your Bible. Don't make excuses. Don't put it off. Just read it!

5. "Grow in the grace and knowledge of our LORD and Savior Jesus Christ" (2 Pet. 3:18). Maturing means two things—growing in grace and growing in knowledge. Growing in grace speaks of dependence on God—trusting Him to provide for your past, present, and future. Growing in knowledge speaks of a hunger to learn more, to strengthen your relationship with your LORD, and to keep on growing and changing.

6. "We are bound to thank God always for you, brethren, as it is fitting, because your faith grows exceedingly, and the love of every one of you all abounds toward each other" (2 Thess. 1:3). The fact that we are growing and maturing shows up in a strong faith and an abounding love for others.

7. "Do not be fooled: You cannot cheat God. People harvest only what they plant. If they plant to satisfy their sinful selves, their sinful selves will bring them ruin. But if they plant to please the Spirit, they will receive eternal life from the Spirit" (Gal. 6:7, 8 NCV).

You reap what you sow, and the only way to encourage growth in our lives is to sow the seeds of righteousness.

8. "If we confess our sins, He is faithful and just to forgive us our sins and to cleanse us from all unrighteousness" (1 John 1:9). Confess and the LORD will forgive. "Afterward Jesus found him in the temple, and said to him, 'See, you have been made well. Sin no more, lest a worse thing come upon you'" (John 5:14). Once you have been forgiven, turn from it and sin no more. Jesus gives you a clean slate and the power to turn away—you are no longer a slave to sin.

9. "Finally, dear brothers and sisters, we urge you in the name of the LORD Jesus to live in a way that pleases God, as we have taught you. You are doing this already, and we encourage you to do so more and more" (1 Thess. 4:1 NLT). If your goal in everything is to please God, you will grow.

Chapter 5

1. "Whoever has the gift of encouraging others should encourage" (Rom. 12:8 NCV). What can we say—it's a gift!

2. "Earnestly desire the best gifts" (1 Cor. 12:31).

3. "Even so you, since you are zealous for spiritual gifts, let it be for the edification of the church that you seek to excel" (1 Cor. 14:12). The gifts are not for our personal gratification, or to add to our resume. They are to be used to edify others.

4. "As each one has received a gift, minister it to one another, as good stewards of the manifold grace of God" (1 Pet. 4:10). God doesn't give useless gifts. His gifts are a perfect fit, practical, and ready to put to work. If we aren't using our gifts, we aren't being wise stewards.

5. "Therefore I remind you to stir up the gift of God which is in you" (2 Tim. 1:6). Other translations say to "kindle afresh," "fan into flames," "rekindle," "let it grow," "keep it ablaze."

6. Barnabas is the most famous encourager in the Bible. "And Joses, who was also named Barnabas by the apostles (which is translated Son of Encouragement), a Levite of the country of Cyprus" (Acts 4:36).

7. "Barnabas was a good man, full of the Holy Spirit and full of faith. When he reached Antioch and saw how God had blessed the people, he was glad. He encouraged all the believers in Antioch always to obey the LORD with all their hearts, and many people became followers of the LORD" (Acts 11:24 NCV). Barnabas, the encourager, is described as good, spirit–filled, full of faith, happy for others, able to exhort, and able to lead others to the LORD.

8. In Acts, we find Paul encouraging many. "Traveling through the country, passing from one gathering to another, he gave constant encouragement, lifting their spirits and charging them with fresh hope" (Acts 20:2 MSG).

9. "And though I have the gift of prophecy, and understand all mysteries and all knowledge, and though I have all faith, so that I could remove mountains, but have not love, I am nothing" (1 Cor. 13:2). We use our gifts to care for and encourage one another because we love one another.

Chapter 6

1. "After the usual readings from the books of Moses and from the Prophets, those in charge of the service sent them this message: 'Brothers, if you have any word of encouragement for us, come and give it!'" (Acts 13:15 NLT). Some translations say "exhortations" or "message of encouragement." Once the Bible had been read aloud to everyone, men were invited to come forward and share. Their testimony encouraged the rest of the congregation.

2. "So when they came out of the jail, they went to Lydia's house where they saw some of the believers and encouraged them. Then they left" (Acts 16:40 NCV). Paul and Silas had just escaped from prison, having been released by a miraculous earthquake. They could have been worried about pursuers, and ducked quickly out of town, but instead they took the time to encourage the believers in that city. Only then did they move on. "When the trouble stopped, Paul sent for the followers to come to him. After he encouraged them and then told them good–bye, he left and went to the country of Macedonia" (Acts 20:1 NCV). This time, Paul had just survived a citywide riot. Though patience was strained and tempers still smoldered, Paul took the time to gather together with the other believers before leaving town.

3. "I am sending to you Tychicus, our brother whom we love and a faithful servant of the LORD's work. He will tell you everything that is happening with me. Then you will know how I am and what I am doing. I am sending him to you for this reason—so that you will know how we are, and he can encourage you" (Eph. 6:21, 22 NCV). Tychicus was sent to share all the news and to encourage his fellow believers. "Tychicus is my dear brother in Christ and a faithful minister and servant with me in the LORD. He will tell you all the things that are happening to me. This is why I am sending him: so you may know how we are and he may encourage you. I send him with Onesimus, a faithful and dear brother in Christ, and one of your group. They will tell you all that has happened here" (Col. 4:7–9 NCV). This time, Paul sent out Tychicus and Onesimus together. Again, they came to bring the people news and to encourage them.

4. "Then, by the will of God, I will be able to come to you with a happy heart, and we will be an encouragement to each other" (Rom. 15:32 NLT). Paul was encouraged when he was able to fellowship with believers. He prayed for the chance to travel and to see his friends again.

5. These trips Paul and his companions took were valuable in many different ways. They allowed believers from different cities and different congregations to receive news of each other. They could share praises and prayer requests. They found out about the miraculous workings of God in cities across whole continents. These trips strengthened their bonds as brothers and sisters in the LORD and gave them opportunities to take up collections for believers in other cities who were struggling financially. People in one city could hear of God's work extending into far away places, and they could rejoice in knowing the Great Commission was being carried out.

6. "His presence was a joy, but so was the news he brought of the encouragement he received from you. When he told me how much you were looking forward to my visit, and how sorry you were about what had happened, and how loyal your love is for me, I was filled with joy!" (2 Cor. 7:7 NLT). Paul enjoyed the companionship of Titus, as well as the news he brought. Paul was especially delighted to hear of his friends' love for him and their anticipation of a visit from him.

7. "They have been a wonderful encouragement to me, as they have been to you, too. You must give proper honor to all who serve so well" (1 Cor. 16:18 NLT). Have you let your encouragers know how much they mean to you? Paul says they deserve proper honor for the good work they do in our hearts.

8. "So, brothers and sisters, while we have much trouble and suffering, we are encouraged about you because of your faith" (1 Thess. 3:7 NCV). Paul was in the midst of "hard times" (MSG) and "crushing troubles" (NLT). Yet when he received the good news of the strong faith in Thessalonica, he did not wonder, "Why not me?" Paul rejoiced because God had blessed them.

9. "Dear brothers and sisters, I close my letter with these last words: Rejoice. Change your ways. Encourage each other. Live in harmony and peace. Then the God of love and peace will be with you" (2 Cor. 13:11 NLT). Often, the P.S. at the end of a letter holds something vitally important. Paul closes his letter with one more reminder to encourage one another.

Chapter 7

1. "And may the LORD make you increase and abound in love to one another and to all, just as we do to you" (1 Thess. 3:12). God is the source of the love we share.

2. "Concerning brotherly love you have no need that I should write to you, for you yourselves are taught by God to love one another" (1 Thess. 4:9). Not only is God the source of the love we share, but He also teaches us how to love. He leads by Christ's example, and He prompts us by the Spirit. Sometimes I think He inspires us with ways to reach out and show love to those who need it most.

3. "These things I command you, that you love one another" (John 15:17). Love is a commandment. "And this is His commandment: that we should believe on the name of His Son Jesus Christ and love one another, as He gave us commandment" (1 John 3:23). God asks that we believe and that we love one another. "For this is the message that you heard from the beginning, that we should love one another" (1 John 3:11). "And now I plead with you, lady, not as though I wrote a new commandment to you, but that which we have had from the beginning: that we love one another" (2 John 1:5). The command to love is nothing new. Jesus told His disciples to do so from the very outset of His ministry. "Beloved, let us love one another, for love is of God; and everyone who loves is born of God and knows God. He who does not love does not know God, for God is love" (1 John 4:7, 8). God is love, and those who know God will have and share that love.

4. "We are all parts of his one body, and each of us has different work to do. And since we are all one body in Christ, we belong to each other, and each of us needs all the others" (Rom. 12:5 NLT). We all belong to Jesus. We belong together. We belong to each other. We need each other. So our love for each other flows out of this unity with Jesus.

5. "With all lowliness and gentleness, with longsuffering, bearing with one another in love" (Eph. 4:2). According to Paul in this verse, we shouldn't act as if we're better than anyone else. We should treat others gently, being considerate of their feelings. We should be longsuffering, willing to have patience in the face of differences. For the sake of love, we should bear with one another, putting up with whatever "stuff" they bring with them.

6. "And above all things have fervent love for one another, for 'love will cover a multitude of sins'" (1 Pet. 4:8). *The Message* puts it this way: "Love makes up for practically anything."

7. "This is My commandment, that you love one another as I have loved you" (John 15:12). We are to love others in the same way God loves us!

8. "Be kindly affectionate to one another with brotherly love, in honor giving preference to one another" (Rom. 12:10). We show our love in affection, but also by putting others ahead of ourselves. We cannot show love when we are being selfish. We must set our wants and needs aside for a while, and give preference to the wants and needs of those we love.

9. "Since you have purified your souls in obeying the truth through the Spirit in sincere love of the brethren, love one another fervently with a pure heart" (1 Pet. 1:22). Love should be fervent—earnest, resolute, passionate, purposeful, and sincere. What's more, our love for each other should come from a pure heart with no hidden agendas or ulterior motives.

10. "No one has ever seen God. But if we love each other, God lives in us, and his love has been brought to full expression through us" (1 John 4:12 NLT). We should not try to harbor God's love, hoarding it for ourselves and holding it back from others. We were meant to be conduits of love, both receiving it and giving it freely. When we share God's love with each other, His love is made perfect. It's the way it was meant to be.

Chapter 8

1. There are so many women our lives touch, and every single one of them who is a believer is our sister in the LORD. These are the "one anothers" the New Testament mentions.

2. "Be of the same mind toward one another" (Rom. 12:16). And "Now may the God of patience and comfort grant you to be like-minded toward one another" (Rom. 15:5). Paul urges believers to be like-minded. Other translations say things like "live in complete harmony with each other" (NLT), "agree with each other," (NCV), and "get along with each other" (MSG). This means that, as sisters, we need to be on the same page. We shouldn't be contradicting each other, trying to thwart each other, and arguing about petty things.

3. "This makes for harmony among the members, so that all the members care for each other equally" (1 Cor. 12:25 NLT). Some members in the body of Christ have more obvious roles than others. Some are seen, while others are unseen and unsung. Paul admonishes us to not give special preference to the more "famous" parts, but to love and appreciate each part equally. Each part is vital to the working of the whole.

4. "Be kind to one another, tenderhearted, forgiving one another, just as God in Christ forgave you" (Eph. 4:32). You should treat your fellow believers with kindness, tenderness, and forgiveness. After all, that is exactly how God treats you!

5. "Be hospitable to one another without grumbling" (1 Pet. 4:9). As believers, we are to be hospitable. No problem! But do we sometimes grumble about it? All the preparations, the cleaning, the cost, the aftermath—aren't they part of the gift? So don't grumble about it! "Do not grumble against one another, brethren, lest you be condemned" (James 5:9).

6. It's the old "Judge not, that you be not judged" (Matt. 7:1). Paul urges, "Let us not judge one another anymore" (Rom. 14:13). As Jesus later says in the Matthew passage, "Why do you look at the speck in your brother's eye, but do not consider the plank in your own eye?" (Matt. 7:3). Don't immerse yourself in what other people are doing. It's not your job to judge their deeds. If they belong to the LORD, He will deal with them.

7. "Have peace with one another" (Mark 9:50).

8. "Submitting to one another in the fear of God" (Eph. 5:21). We are to be submissive. "All of you be submissive to one another, and be clothed with humility, for 'God resists the proud, but gives grace to the humble'" (1 Pet. 5:5). We shouldn't set ourselves up as better than anyone else. We are to be humble and serve one another. We are to be "down to earth with each other" (1 Pet. 5:5 MSG).

9. "Bearing with one another, and forgiving one another, if anyone has a complaint against another; even as Christ forgave you, so you also must do" (Col. 3:13). Once again, we see a common thread continue. Bear with one another and put up with each other for the sake of God. Practice forgiving one another instead of complaining about each other, because this is how Jesus has treated us.

Chapter 9

1. "Bear one another's burdens, and so fulfill the law of Christ" (Gal. 6:2). In the words of a few other translations: "Share each other's troubles and problems" (NLT), "helping each other with your troubles" (NCV), "stoop down and reach out to those who are oppressed" (MSG).

2. "Putting away lying, 'Let each one of you speak truth with his neighbor,' for we are members of one another" (Eph. 4:25). And then, "Do not lie to one another, since you have put off the old man with his deeds" (Col. 3:9). We are called to be honest women.

3. Two very good reasons for being truthful are given in these verses: First, we should be honest because we are all members of God's family. Second, we should be truthful because lying is a sin, and we are to put away all the doings of our old nature.

4. "Receive one another, just as Christ also received us, to the glory of God" (Rom. 15:7). We are asked to receive one another, welcome one another, and accept one another.

5. "If I then, your LORD and Teacher, have washed your feet, you also ought to wash one another's feet" (John 13:14). Are you willing to set aside your pride, inhibitions, and even your dignity in order to serve? If Jesus was able to take on the role of a servant, couldn't you do so as well?

6. "Through love serve one another" (Gal. 5:13). This can be hard both ways. For those of us who are of an independent nature, we don't feel we need the help. For those of us who find it hard to stoop to work we feel beneath us, we would rather not be pressed into service.

7. "Do not speak evil of one another, brethren" (James 4:11). This means no gossip, no slander, and no backstabbing. Your words were not meant to cut one another down, but instead to bless and encourage.

8. "Let us not become conceited, provoking one another, envying one another" (Gal. 5:26). These sound like a cropping up of sibling rivalry: provoking, teasing, taunting, insulting, slandering, envying, behaving selfishly, coveting, and feeling we are being treated unfairly.

9. "Now I myself am confident concerning you, my brethren, that you also are full of goodness, filled with all knowledge, able also to admonish one another" (Rom. 15:14).

We should be able to gently admonish one another. That means we have soaked up so much of the goodness and knowledge of the Word, we are able to teach one another about our faith. "Speaking to one another in psalms and hymns and spiritual songs, singing and making melody in your heart to the LORD" (Eph. 5:19). "Let the word of Christ dwell in you richly in all wisdom, teaching and admonishing one another in psalms and hymns and spiritual songs, singing with grace in your hearts to the LORD" (Col. 3:16). This verse says God's Word should dwell in us, and it is out of the grace in our hearts we sing.

Chapter 10

1. "I weep; tears flow down my cheeks. No one is here to comfort me; any who might encourage me are far away" (Lam. 1:16 NLT). How could Jeremiah be encouraged when there was no one to help him? With all of his friends so far away, he was left without the comfort of encouragement.

2. "And from there, when the brethren heard about us, they came to meet us as far as Appii Forum and Three Inns. When Paul saw them, he thanked God and took courage" (Acts 28:15). Paul must have been a little bit nervous about his upcoming trial in Rome. But good news travels fast, and the believers in Rome found out he was coming. Their "welcome wagon" efforts not only encouraged Paul, but gave him courage as well.

3. "And truly you do love the Christians in all of Macedonia. Brothers and sisters, now we encourage you to love them even more" (1 Thess. 4:10 NCV). Christianity is not meant to be a series of cliques. Our care and encouragement for fellow believers need not stop with those we have met.

4. "So encourage each other and give each other strength, just as you are doing now" (1 Thess. 5:11 NCV). Our encouragement gives others the strength to carry on, strength to grow, and strength to rejoice through our days. Other translations say our encouragement for one another can "edify," "build up," and more specifically, "Build up hope so you'll all be together in this, no one left out, no one left behind" (1 Thess. 5:11 MSG).

5. "Take tender care of those who are weak. Be patient with everyone" (1 Thess. 5:14 NLT). Paul urges believers to reach out to those who need encouragement the most—those who are weak, exhausted, and straggling behind. When your sister is struggling with life and faith, yours can be the hand that helps her to her feet and supports her along the path for a while.

6. "Worry weighs a person down; an encouraging word cheers a person up" (Prov. 12:25 NLT). A word of encouragement can often drive away the worries that tend to plague us.

7. "Don't use foul or abusive language. Let everything you say be good and helpful, so that your words will be an encouragement to those who hear them" (Eph. 4:29 NLT). Your words can build up or they can tear down. Paul asks us to choose our words carefully, so they will encourage and strengthen one another.

8. "Think about the many people you have taught and the weak hands you have made strong. Your words have comforted those who fell, and you have strengthened those who could not stand" (Job 4:3, 4 NCV). Job wisely strengthened those who were weak and comforted those who failed. He did not discard those who couldn't keep up, but helped them until they could do their part again. In *The Message*, it says Job "encouraged those who were about to quit."

9. "Let this encourage God's holy people to endure persecution patiently and remain firm to the end, obeying his commands and trusting in Jesus" (Rev. 14:12 NLT). Encouragement can help us to hang in there, patiently enduring persecution, standing steadfast no matter what, and remaining obedient until the end.

Chapter 11

1. "I have written this short letter to you with the help of Silas, whom I consider a faithful brother. My purpose in writing is to encourage you and assure you that the grace of God is with you no matter what happens" (1 Pet. 5:12 NLT). The epistle writers of the New Testament were writing to encourage the faith of the early believers.

2. "I write to you, fathers, Because you have known Him who is from the beginning. I write to you, young men, Because you have overcome the wicked one. I write to you, little children, Because you have known the Father" (1 John 2:13). That's us! We know Jesus. We know the Father. We are overcomers!

3. "My brothers and sisters, I beg you to listen patiently to this message I have written to encourage you, because it is not very long" (Heb. 13:22 NCV). Encouragement is in the Bible for the taking, but in order to find it, you must read the letters, and you must accept their teaching. It was the same for the original recipients of these encouraging epistles.

4. "If anyone thinks himself to be a prophet or spiritual, let him acknowledge that the things which I write to you are the commandments of the LORD" (1 Cor. 14:37). It was understood Paul spoke for God, and that God spoke through Paul. Paul had the authority of apostleship, and the believers respected his words as truth.

5. "Having confidence in your obedience, I write to you, knowing that you will do even more than I say" (Philem. 1:21). Paul is so confident of his friendship with Philemon, he was sure he would fulfill his request—and more.

6. "For me to write the same things to you is not tedious, but for you it is safe" (Phil. 3:1). Paul knew the repetition was necessary, because we would need it. By hearing the same themes over again, we are able to grasp them firmly and apply them effectively to our lives. It's not tedious. It's helping us to stay prepared.

7. "These things I write to you, though I hope to come to you shortly" (1 Tim. 3:14). Paul longed to be reunited with his good friend. "I had many things to write, but I do not wish to write to you with pen and ink; but I hope to see you shortly, and we shall speak face to face" (3 John 1:13, 14). John wanted to see his friends face to face. "Having many things to write to you, I did not wish to do so with paper and ink; but I hope to come to you and speak face to face, that our joy may be full" (2 John 1:12). Whether in person or by letter, words from a dear friend bring joy and encouragement to our hearts.

8. c, d, e, h, a, f, g, b.

9. "The salutation of Paul with my own hand, which is a sign in every epistle; so I write" (2 Thess. 3:17). Paul closed each of his encouraging epistles with his own brief message and signature. This was a way for the readers to authenticate the message, and assure themselves the letter was not a forgery. Some say Paul's penmanship was something of an "inside joke" among the Christians, because his failing eyesight forced him to write in a large, almost childlike script. This is suggested in Galatians 6:11, where Paul gleefully declares, "See with what large letters I have written to you with my own hand!"

10. "You are our epistle written in our hearts, known and read by all men; clearly you are an epistle of Christ, ministered by us, written not with ink but by the Spirit of the living God, not on tablets of stone but on tablets of flesh, that is, of the heart" (2 Cor. 3:2, 3). The believers in the churches Paul visited were living testimonials of the effectiveness of Paul's ministry. They were the proof that God was using Paul. They were witnesses to God's power and Paul's faithfulness.

Chapter 12

1. "Me? Encourage others? I'm the one who needs to be encouraged!" Selfishness and self–centeredness stand in the way of effective encouragement. "I can't afford it." "I don't have time!" "I'm not organized enough." Often we drag our feet in avenues of ministry because we think we have to have everything pulled together before we begin. Though planning can make your service more intentional, you can give your sister a little lift any time the opportunity presents itself. Just do it!

2. A little brainstorming is all it takes to realize there are dozens of ways to offer encouragement to those we know. As Christian women, we are part of a community. God urges us to use our gifts to show His love to those around us. It was this very love Jesus spoke of when He said others would recognize His followers because of the love they showed for one another (John 13:35). Open your eyes and heart. Look for areas of need. Then take a few minutes to share God's love.

3. The first day of spring calls for daffodils. Buy a bunch or cut your own, then hand them out to your friends. Or maybe a couple of you can grab a mop and bucket and help a friend out with her spring–cleaning. Or offer to go to her office with her and do the filing. The first day of summer could be celebrated with some sunglasses from the dollar store or a packet of seeds or a beach ball. Celebrate autumn by pressing leaves in your phone book, then mailing them to friends with messages on them. Or maybe you can have a bulb–planting party, and put in crocuses, tulips, and hyacinths for a friend. The first day of winter would be the perfect time to send a new box of tea or a cassette tape of seasonal music. Why not arrange to take a friend window–shopping, then visit over coffee or cocoa.

4. Call your best friend and sing "Me and My Shadow" to her on Groundhog's Day. Send "little kids" valentines to your sisters for the first two weeks of February—one every day. Collect enough green things to fill a shoebox, and mail it to someone special in March. Grown–ups love egg hunts too, so why not host one for all your friends. It's encouraging to do thoughtful things together, so get together a group and make May baskets for all the recluses in your church. Send your favorite picnic/potluck recipe in time for the Fourth of July. Hand out pretty gourds or baby pumpkins in October. A brand new wooden spoon tied up with a bow will help get Thanksgiving dinner off to a good start. December calls for cocoa mix and marshmallows and a new Christmas cookie cutter or two. Make the girls laugh with some silly New Year's resolutions, like "I resolve to name everything on my desk this year, in order to improve our working relationship."

5. Tuck an envelope of instant soup mix into a card for January's little lift. Hang pinecones dipped in peanut butter and rolled in birdseed near your friends' windows in February. Go for a walk in the rain in March. Take a buddy to a Mexican restaurant in May, where you can eat chips and salsa and split an order of fajitas. Send a buddy some tea bags and your favorite fruit tea recipe in June. Host a weenie roast in July. Do a cheese–tasting party in August. Make a chicken potpie for your girlfriend's freezer in September. In October, make a gift basket with a jar of popcorn, a stick of butter, and a shaker of salt. Give peanut butter cookies to everyone you love in November. And in December, send an encouraging note scrawled on the back of a homemade bingo card.

6. Plan a tea party in April during National Straw Hat week, and make sure every lady in attendance has a flowery bowery chapeau for the day. Send all your friends pennies in February for Lost Penny Day. In May, have a limerick writing party, and see who can come up with the zaniest rhyme: "I once knew a Meberg named Marilyn, who decided to go Christmas carolin'. So with Luci in tow, and a sled for the snow, they swooshed into town, simply barrelin'." Encourage your girlfriends to throw in the dishtowel on No Housework Day. Send out bubble bath and rubber duckies for National Bathtub Party Day. It'd be fun!

7. For my niece's fourth birthday, I wanted to send something more memorable than a card. We had just moved far away, so I used one of the big moving boxes to send her a care package. For just ninety–nine cents apiece, I bought four big helium birthday balloons—the Mylar ones that last for several days. They filled the box without weighing it down much, so postage only cost four dollars. Their whole family got a surprise when that box was opened and the balloons tumbled up to the ceiling! It doesn't take a lot of time or money to put together a little gift box for someone. Padded envelopes are wonderful inventions and they now come in pretty patterns and colors. A care package is a personalized present is designed to lift the heart of someone, no matter what the need.

8. "Let us consider one another in order to stir up love and good works" (Heb. 10:24). We are urged to be thoughtful, to consider one another. Encouragement cannot come if we are too absorbed in our own lives to notice the needs of others. "Not forsaking the assembling of ourselves together" (Heb. 10:25). We need to cultivate our relationships with one another. After all, we can only meet the needs we know about! When we gather together, we are able to encourage one another in our walk with the LORD.

9. As with many other things, the easiest place to start practicing the ministry of encouragement is in your own home. Why not begin by lifting the spirits of those you know and love best. Friends, neighbors, family members, even strangers will benefit from your commitment to show God's love in encouraging ways to those you meet. Go for it!

✦ ACKNOWLEDGMENTS ✦

© Clairmont, Patsy, *The Best Devotions of Patsy Clairmont,* (Grand Rapids, MI: Zondervan Publishing House, 2001)

© Johnson, Barbara, *Daily Splashes of Joy,* (Nashville, TN: W Publishing Group, 2000)

© Johnson, Nicole, *Fresh–Brewed Life: A Stirring Invitation to Wake up Your Soul,* (Nashville, TN: Thomas Nelson, Inc., 2001)

© Johnson, Nicole, *Keeping a Princess Heart in a Not–So–Fairy–Tale World,* (Nashville, TN: W Publishing Group, 2003)

© Meberg, Marilyn, *The Best Devotions of Marilyn Meberg* (Grand Rapids, MI: Zondervan Publishing House, 2001)

© Swindoll, Luci, *I Married Adventure* (Nashville, TN: W Publishing Group, 2003)

© Walsh, Sheila, *The Best Devotions of Sheila Walsh and Unexpected Grace* (Grand Rapids, MI: Zondervan Publishing House, 2001)

© Wells, Thelma, *The Best Devotions of Thelma Wells* (Grand Rapids, MI: Zondervan Publishing House, 2001)

✦ STATEMENT OF FAITH ✦

Women of Faith believes...

The Bible to be the inspired, the only infallible, inerrant Word of God.

There is one God, eternally existent in three persons: Father, Son, and Holy Spirit.

He has revealed Himself in creation, history and Jesus Christ.

God's creation of the world and humankind with humanity's rebellion and subsequent depravity.

In the person and work of Jesus Christ, including His deity,

His virgin birth, His sinless life, His true humanity, His miracles,

His substitutionary death, His bodily resurrection,

His ascension to heaven, and His personal return in power and glory.

That for salvation of the lost, sinful man, regeneration by the Holy Spirit is absolutely essential.

Salvation is by grace through faith in Christ as one's Savior.

In the present ministry of the Holy Spirit by whose indwelling the Christian is enabled to live a godly life and to grow in the knowledge of God and Christian obedience.

In the resurrection of both the saved and the lost—the saved unto the resurrection of life and the lost unto the resurrection of damnation.

In the spiritual unity of believers in the LORD Jesus Christ and in the importance of church for worship, service and missions.

✦ NOTES ✦

✦ NOTES ✦

WOMEN OF FAITH
A Division of Thomas Nelson, Inc.

PRESENTS

Irrepressible
HOPE
CONFERENCE 2004

Featured Speakers & Dramatist:

Sheila Walsh

Marilyn Meberg

Luci Swindoll

Patsy Clairmont

Thelma Wells

Nicole Johnson

There is more to life than just staying afloat!
Experience the all-new two day conference that can put fresh wind in your sails — with stirring music, engaging dramatic presentations and refreshing messages.

We have this hope as an anchor for the soul, firm and secure.

—HEBREWS 6:19

2004 Event Cities and Special Guests

Shreveport, LA
February 27-28
CenturyTel Center

Philadelphia, PA - I
March 5-6
Wachovia Spectrum

San Antonio, TX*
March 18-20
AlamoDome

Ft. Wayne, IN
March 26-27
Allen County
War Memorial
Coliseum- Arena

Spokane, WA
April 16-17
Spokane Arena

Cincinnati, OH
April 23-24
US Bank Arena

San Jose, CA
May 7-8
HP Pavilion

Nashville, TN
May 14-15
Gaylord Entertainment
Center

Charleston, SC
May 21-22
N. Charleston Coliseum

Des Moines, IA
June 4-5
Veterans Memorial
Auditorium

Anaheim, CA - I
June 18-19
Arrowhead Pond

Pittsburgh, PA
June 25-26
Mellon Arena

Denver, CO
July 9-10
Pepsi Center

Ft. Lauderdale, FL
July 16-17
Office Depot Center

St. Louis, MO
July 23-24
Savvis Center

Atlanta, GA
July 30-31
Philips Arena

Washington, DC
August 6-7
MCI Center

Buffalo, NY
August 13-14
HSBC Arena

Omaha, NE
August 20-21
Qwest Center Omaha

Dallas, TX
August 27-28
American Airlines Center

Anaheim, CA - II
September 10-11
Arrowhead Pond

Albany, NY
September 17-18
Pepsi Arena

Philadelphia, PA - II
September 24-25
Wachovia Center

Hartford, CT
October 1-2
Hartford Civic Center

Portland, OR
October 8-9
Rose Garden Arena

Orlando, FL
October 15-16
TD Waterhouse Centre

St. Paul, MN
October 22-23
Xcel Energy Center

Charlotte, NC
October 29-30
Charlotte Coliseum

Oklahoma City, OK
November 5-6
Ford Center

Vancouver, BC
November 12-13
GM Place

Dates and locations subject to change.

* Special National Conference. Call 1-888-49-FAITH for details.

For more information call **1-888-49-FAITH** or visit **womenoffaith.com**

The Complete Women of Faith® Study Guide Series

Discovering God's
Will for Your Life
0-7852-4983-4

Living Above
Worry and Stress
0-7852-4986-9

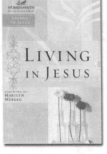

Living in Jesus
0-7852-4985-0

Adventurous
Prayer
0-7852-4984-2

NEW RELEASES

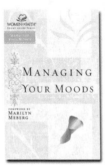

Managing
Your Moods
0-7852-5151-0

Cultivating
Contentment
0-7852-5152-9

Encouraging
One Another
0-7852-5153-7

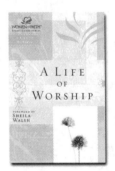

A Life of Worship
0-7852-5154-5

WOMEN OF FAITH®

A Message of Grace & Hope
for Every Day

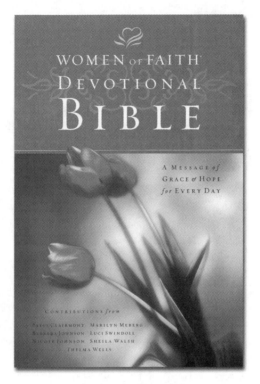

Hardcover: 0-7180-0378-0
Paperback: 0-7180-0377-2
Bonded Leather: 0-7180-0379-9

The *Women of Faith® Devotional Bible* provides women with the inspiration and resources needed to strengthen their walk with God and build stronger relationships with others. It helps women of all ages and stages in life – mature believers and those who have yet to believe, from all backgrounds, church and non-churched — to grow spiritually, emotionally, and relationally.